W9-AKT-231

Woodworking Projects for the Kitchen

Woodworking Projects for the Kitchen

50 Useful, Easy-to-Make Items

Mark Strom
& Lee Rankin

A Sterling/Lark Book
Sterling Publishing Co., Inc.   New York

Editor: Chris Rich

Art Director: Chris Colando

Production: Elaine Thompson, Chris Colando, Charlie Covington

Illustrations: Don Osby

Photography: Evan Bracken

Library of Congress Cataloging-in-Publication Data
Strom, Mark.
    Woodworking projects for the kitchen : 50 useful, easy-to-make
items / by Mark Strom & Lee Rankin.
        p.   cm.
    "A Sterling/Lark book."
    Includes index..
    ISBN 0-8069-0396-1
    1. Woodwork.   2. Kitchen utensils.   3. Furniture making.
    I. Rankin, Lee, 1945-   .   II. Title
    TT200.S74   1993
    684'.08--dc20   93-17314
                                                         CIP

10 9 8 7 6 5 4 3 2 1

A Sterling/Lark Book

Produced by Altamont Press, Inc.
50 College St., Asheville, NC 28801

Published in 1993 by Sterling Publishing Co., Inc.
387 Park Avenue S., New York, NY 10016

© 1993, Altamont Press

Distributed in Canada by Sterling Publishing,
c/o Canadian Manda Group, P.O. Box 920, Station U, Toronto,
Ontario M8Z 5P9

Distributed in the United Kingdom by Cassell PLC, Villiers House,
41/47 Strand, London WC2N 5JE, England

Distributed in Australia by Capricorn Link, Ltd., P.O. Box 665,
Lane Cove, NSW 2066

Every effort has been made to ensure that all information in this
book is accurate. However, due to differing conditions, tools,
and individual skills, the publisher cannot be responsible for any
injuries, losses, or other damages which may result from the use
of the information in this book.

All rights reserved.

Printed in Hong Kong

ISBN 0-8069-0396-1

Table of Contents

Introduction

This book is for you if

- ◆ you've always envied those designer kitchens, with their emphasis on the richness and warmth of wood.

- ◆ your eyes have ever glazed over in a department store as you searched for a kitchen item made of something other than plastic.

- ◆ your kitchen could use more display space or an attractive accessory that's functional and beautiful.

- ◆ you're depressed by the poor quality and high cost of ready-made kitchenware.

- ◆ you panic every time you need to select a gift for someone special.

In today's world of mass-produced kitchenware, much of it apparently created to self-destruct, wood adds a special sense of permanence and history to the home. It's appealing to the eye, comforting to the touch, and durable. And most important of all, wood is accessible. You don't have to be a master woodworker to improve your kitchen (or someone else's) with the warmth and personality of a fine, wood-crafted item. Anyone who has a basic knowledge of woodworking tools and techniques, a standard set of tools, and a few hours' time, can leave desperate shopping trips and ugly kitchens behind. Even if your woodworking skills are practically nonexistent, take heart! You'll find projects within these pages that are well within your reach.

With a few exceptions, these projects are small; they'll last a lifetime or longer, but not one of them will take a lifetime to build. And because they're small, they're also adaptable; you won't have to rearrange the furniture or move a cabinet to make room for your completed work. From traditional cutting boards and simple shelves to contemporary, under-the-cupboard stemware racks, every item was designed to enhance—not drastically alter—your existing kitchen's looks and operation.

The first part of this book offers thorough, up-to-date descriptions of the required tools and techniques. You'll also find helpful sections on selecting projects, organizing your workshop, and ensuring your personal safety as you work. Browse through this introductory material even if you're a pro; it's never too late to learn something new. As you skim through the projects, take a look at the lists provided with each. These will save you both time and money—time spent on shopping and money spent on unnecessary materials, tools, hardware, and supplies.

Once you're ready to begin building, step-by-step instructions and detailed illustrations will walk you through every step of the construction process. To give you some idea of what these projects will do for a kitchen's decor, we've also included color photographs of many finished pieces in their kitchen settings; use these photos, by all means, as you decide where your own projects will look their best.

Why spend hours on fruitless shopping trips or thousands of dollars redecorating, when a carefully selected and lovingly shaped trivet or step stool can make even an ordinary kitchen look special? All you need to do is decide what to build and then set aside a day or two in which to build it. In fact, the only disadvantage to beginning one of these projects is that you may not be able to stop once you've finished it! Wood is just as fascinating to work with as it is to see and touch, and once the woodworking "bug" has bitten you, you may never kick the pleasure it brings.

First
Steps

PLANNING

Whether you intend to make something special for your own kitchen or construct a project for someone else's, a few minutes invested in pre-construction planning will double your enjoyment of the finished product. Nothing is more frustrating than hastily building something, only to discover that the results don't match your needs or expectations. The Over-the-Sink Cutting Board, for instance, looks great, but if it doesn't fit over *your* sink, you might end up wishing you'd chosen the Traditional Cutting Board instead!

Based on the woodworking mistakes we've made ourselves, we've compiled a list of questions that we wish we'd thought to answer before we picked up a square or saw. The answers you give to these same questions will help you to decide what you'd like to add to your kitchen—and why.

◆ Where will I put the item that
I'd like to build?

Beware of immediate answers like "on the kitchen counter," or "on the wall next to the door." When it's excited about woodworking, the imagination has an amazing capacity to invent space that isn't really there! Your kitchen counters—the same ones now occupied by entire colonies of small appliances—suddenly become vast, empty deserts. Walls—the ones that are hidden every time you open a door—cry out for decorative racks and shelves. You forget that you own and adore a dog—who owns and adores that corner where you'd love to put a butcher block table.

We strongly recommend that you measure the actual counter top, wall, or floor space that you have in mind. Then compare the measurements you take with those given in the project's illustration. What do your calculations tell you? Will the project really fit where you'd like to put it? Will you be able to reach it easily? Will it show? The more realistic you can be now, the happier you'll be later.

◆ What will this project look like once
I've set it up in its new location?

One way to find out is to carry this book straight to the kitchen and study the color photographs while you're there. Look closely at your kitchen woodwork—windows, doors, trim, and cabinets. Does the wood that we recommend clash in any way with the wood that's already there? If so, select a wood that suits your present decor; our recommendations aren't written in stone. What about the project's size? You might be able to squeeze that Adjustable Cookbook Stand into the space you've chosen, but will it make your kitchen look cluttered instead of cared for?

◆ How long will this project take
to build?

We're tempted to tell you that most of these kitchen accessories can be constructed in a weekend or less, but individual schedules and temperaments would probably make liars of us. Uninterrupted blocks of time are just plain hard to come by. As soon as you promise yourself a weekend alone in the workshop, surprise visitors knock on the door, the basement floods, or the boss demands overtime.

So what's the answer? Half of it lies in the way we've designed most of these projects—so that you can easily stop and then start again without ruining what you've already done. The other half rests with you. Relax! Let the inevitable pauses refresh you, and if you need to, remind yourself that woodworking can and should be just as much fun as using what you make. If your everyday life is especially harried, choose an easy project like the Mug Rack—one you can make so quickly that you'll barely have time to be distracted.

◆ Will I use what I've built?

We like to use what we build. Not long ago, however, we realized that some people enjoy displaying useful objects, instead of putting them to work. Ornaments in the kitchen—beautiful, functional, but rarely used objects—have a long and respectable history, so we've stopped assuming that there's only one answer to this question. Some people will want to focus on building projects that they know will help them with everyday kitchen tasks. Others may prefer to display their handi-work. Still others may want to make things to give as gifts. No matter which group you belong to, you'll find a project here to please you.

◆ How much will it cost to undertake this venture?

We can't answer this one for you, but we can give you a head start on finding an answer for yourself. First, take a look at the materials and hardware lists that come with every project. Then call your local lumberyard (or specialty-wood supplier) and your hardware store to get current prices. Keep in mind that if you intend to build more than a single project, buying in bulk may save you money. Consider renting or borrowing tools that you don't already own. Treat our materials recommendations as suggestions, not as commands; if you need to substi-tute a less expensive wood species, go right ahead.

◆ Am I skilled enough to tackle this project?

Though none of the ones in this book are complex, many require some degree of familiarity with woodwork-ing tools. Don't be daunted if you're a beginner, though. Start by selecting a project that strikes you as fairly sim-ple. Read through its instructions carefully, visualizing each step as you do. When you run into a tool or wood-working term that's completely unfamiliar to you, look up what you need to know in the chapter entitled Tools and Techniques. Then, before you attempt the actual project, practice the techniques on scrap wood.

Once you've taken these preparatory steps, consider ask-ing a woodworking friend to give you a hand as you work. Or plunge right in; there's no teacher like experience!

THE WORKSHOP

Good cooks—and good woodworkers—know that at least one key to success is the space in which they work. Of course, you can bake a tasty potato or build a functional birdhouse while you're standing in the great outdoors, but even though our kitchen projects won't require an elaborate or costly workshop, you will need to build them indoors. Your shop should be dry, well ventilated, and well lit, and you'll also need a work-bench.

Your bench will provide a level work surface where you can glue, drill, and rout your stock, and it will also serve as a base for a vise. A good bench is really solid; the heavier it is, the less likely it will be to shift as you work. You can prevent potential shifting by placing the bench against a solid wall, but your best bet is to buy or build a solid bench instead. Workbenches of high quali-ty will include dogs, a vise, a tool well, and stretchers between the legs for extra support, but don't worry if yours lacks these extras. For your comfort and working ease, make sure that your bench is hip-height.

Keeping your workshop organized is easy. Just desig-nate a home for every object in it, and when you're fin-ished using that object, send it back where it belongs. Some woodworkers keep their most frequently used tools visible; pegboards work well for this purpose. With a marker, outline each tool's shape while it's on the board. Later, a quick glance at the board will remind you where each tool belongs. Label shelves and draw-ers, too. Eventually, you'll no longer need these clean-up cues, but in the meantime they'll make great time-saving devices.

Avoid buying expensive tools unless you're sure you'll use them frequently. Don't buy shoddy ones either: they won't last, they may not work well, and they're sometimes even unsafe. Rent or borrow tools instead. When you're ready to purchase, though, always buy the very best tools that you can afford; in the long run, they'll save you money. Look after them by clean-ing them, keeping them rust-free, and following the manufacturer's instructions regarding their use, maintenance, and repair.

SAFETY

Sure, ignoring basic safety rules can sometimes shave a few minutes off a time-consuming workshop procedure. But the old saw about haste making waste makes especially good sense when you work with wood. Wasting a project by making haste in the shop isn't a tragedy; wasting a limb or a life is. Take the time to stick to the rules that follow, and you'll live to be glad you did!

◆ Your body and mind need to be calm and rested when you work with wood. If they're not, vent your hostilities or take a nap before—not after—you enter your shop. Your project can wait.

◆ The moving parts of a power tool don't pick and choose what they slice, bore, or sand—they take whatever is put in their path, including loose clothing, watch bands, necklaces, rings, and parts of the human body. You don't have to strip or shave your head, but do change into close-fitting clothes, and tie back or tuck up your hair before you start work. Be conscious of every movement you make and of its possible consequences.

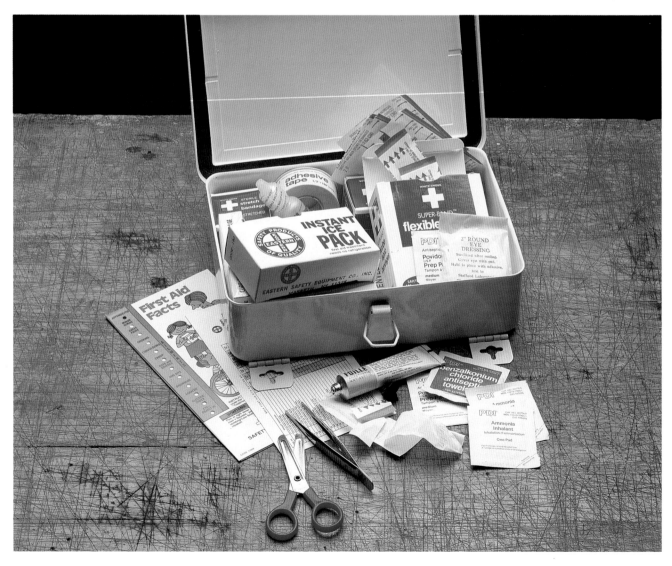

◆ Blade guards guard you, not the blades they cover. Sometimes they're omitted from the photographs in a book, but only to show you parts or processes that can't be seen otherwise. Keep them where they belong! As an extra precaution, never stand directly behind or in front of a moving blade, even when the guard is where it should be. The blade is unlikely to jump out of its mounting, but anything it flings—a wood chip, for instance—may be moving at a lethal speed.

◆ Purchase double-insulated tools or ground them, and don't use power tools when your feet are anywhere near water. Before you adjust any of your tools or change bits or blades, unplug the cord, and check the cords frequently, too.

◆ Workshop fires are much too easy to start. Don't smoke around sawdust, oils, and finishes, or use power tools when flammable gases are in the air. Keep your shop clean, and make sure there's a fire extinguisher handy.

◆ When you're working with volatile substances, use an exhaust fan to pull tainted air away from you, and wear a respirator that's designed to filter out noxious fumes. A dust mask won't do this job, though it will keep airborne particles like sawdust out of your lungs.

◆ Place trash—especially sawdust, wood scraps, and finish-soaked rags—in a covered, metal container. Empty it regularly. Keep all horizontal surfaces, including the floor, free of anything that might catch in a

moving bit or blade or that might cause you to slip.

◆ Make sure your ear plugs or protectors are in or on when volume levels rise above normal. Protect your eyes with goggles; woodworkers who wear them may look screamingly funny, but they don't lose their eyesight in workshop accidents.

◆ Children as young as seven years old can learn the basics of woodworking, but not when they're in a shop alone and not while you're too busy to supervise. Unless you're prepared to spend time working with them on their own projects, protect your children by keeping your workshop door locked.

◆ Accidents don't have to happen. When they do, though, you'll be awfully glad that you have a first-aid kit. Check it regularly and keep it well stocked.

UNDERSTANDING WOOD

Wood isn't likely to go out of fashion anytime soon. It's warm, workable, and as varied as its grain and colors. But it also keeps secrets from those who aren't familiar with it. Though you won't need to memorize this section, the information in it will help you to purchase and use your wood wisely.

The elements (or extractives) in woods yield each wood's various properties, including color, density, and strength, and are what distinguish one type of wood from another. Wood species are classified as hardwoods or softwoods, depending upon the extractives in them.

Most of the hardwoods and softwoods used in these kitchen projects should be available from a retail lumberyard or a home improvement center. Some of the less common species, however, may have to be ordered through a millwork or specialty supplier. Commercial softwoods such as pine are readily available, reasonably priced, and easy to work with. Because strength is not a major factor for the kitchen items in this book, you can use any clear-grade softwood when you build them.

The hardwoods—oak, maple, cherry, walnut, birch, and poplar—are more expensive, stronger, and often more attractive than softwood species. They're also more difficult to work with simply because they're harder, but sharp blades and tool bits will minimize this disadvantage.

Unless you have access to a custom sawmill, the wood you purchase will meet the standards of the industry. If you've ever wondered why those standards mean that the 1 x 2s you see in the lumberyard are really only 3/4" x 1-1/2", an explanation follows!

Commercial softwoods are sized and priced by their rough mill-sawn (or nominal) dimensions—1 x 2, for example. But when the raw stock is planed down, as it needs to be for the marketplace, its mill-sawn size can be reduced by as much as 25 percent. By the time you buy a nominal 1 x 2 at the building supply store, its "actual" dimensions are closer to 3/4" x 1-1/2". You'll find a list of nominal and actual softwood sizes on page 151.

A piece of softwood less than 1" thick and between 2" and 6" wide is called a strip; wood less than 2" thick and up to 16" wide falls into the board category. Standard lengths run from 6' to 16', in two-foot increments.

Hardwood boards come in random widths up to 6". Their thickness is measured in 1/4" graduations, from 1" to 4", and is expressed as a fraction. The 4/4 (pronounced "four-quarter") boards used in many of these projects measure 1" before they're planed down to 13/16" for the market. Lengths range from 4' to 16'.

Hardwood can be sold as rough, when it hasn't been planed, and as surfaced, after it's been planed on one or more sides. The project wood most readily available is called S2S because it's been surfaced on two sides.

Hardwood is sold in volume by the board foot, a long-standing measure by which each unit is equivalent to a rough board measuring 1" thick by 12" wide by 12" long—144 cubic inches all told. Any stock less than 1" thick is counted as a full inch, and anything over 1" is figured to the next larger 1/4". A 6'-long 1 x 6 therefore contains three board feet, and so does a piece measuring 1-3/8" x 2" by 12'. To figure board feet, multiply thickness by width in inches; then multiply by length in feet and divide by 12.

Lumber is "graded" (or categorized) by a variety of physical standards and then further graded by use. Softwoods, including pine, are graded as either finish or select. The select grades, which include shelving and trim stock, are B & Better (commonly known as 1 and 2 Clear), and C Select, which contains limited defects.

Hardwood lumber is graded differently. Firsts and Seconds (FAS) comprise the best grade; the boards are at least 6" wide and 8' long. Selects (the next grade down the scale) are FAS-quality boards at least 4" wide and 6' in length. Shorts, or No. 1 Common, is limited to a minimum 3" width and 4' length, and is the least expensive project wood.

When you select wood for your projects, cost and appearance will probably play an important role. Check the look of the wood that you want before you buy it. Watch for knotholes, surface imperfections, warpage, and for checks or cracks. In hardwoods, where you're paying for appearance, be especially critical of pith (soft spots), stain, and insect holes. Some lumberyards try to discourage "hand-picking." When you encounter this problem, shop somewhere else! There's no reason to pay for something that doesn't meet your standards.

Don't, however, be overly concerned about the wood's workability. Every species we've recommended (except poplar) will cut cleanly if you use sharp tools. Poplar may suffer some "tear-out," but that can easily be sanded away. Oak, maple, and birch can be stubbornly hard but are workable.

The final decision that you make regarding which woods to use may end up being a simple matter of economics. Who'd pass over a stack of birch at a bargain for a few costly pieces of walnut or cherry? And why? A carefully built birch project will probably look a lot better than one constructed sloppily with a more expensive wood.

Tools and Techniques

Unless you plan to build all 50 projects, you won't need to read this chapter word-for-word. Treat it, instead, as a useful reference. When the project that you've chosen requires a tool with which you're not familiar, or you're not sure which technique to use, just skim through these pages for the basic information you need. If you're a newcomer to the world of woodworking, you may want to shore up your confidence by reading the sections that apply to the required tools for your selected project. And more experienced woodworkers may want to browse through our descriptions and explanations, if only to brush up on techniques that are too often taken for granted.

Whether you're a novice or an expert, however, keep in mind that your most important tool is yourself. A state-of-the-art workshop is only as effective as you make it, so don't fall into the expensive trap of thinking that the tools make the woodworker. If you don't know how to use them, they'll only make you poor! When you purchase new tools, invest in the best, but remember that a good woodworker can make a few standard tools work wonders.

One hint before you begin: Hang on to the instructional inserts that come with new tools. Not surprisingly, some of the useful tips they provide will make better sense to you once you've used your tools enough to understand their structure and function. Practice using any new tool, too. Get a feel for how it handles by trying it out on some scrap wood. These trial runs will not only improve your skills but will also test your new equipment before its warranty expires!

CLAMPING AND HOLDING

Clamps are used to grip parts to each other or to a bench so that you can mark, drill, or cut them; they also serve to hold glued parts together as the glue dries. Used with strips of wood, clamps can be transformed into saw and router guides or extended over enlarged areas. Of the many types of clamps manufactured, the ones you'll need for these projects are C-clamps and bar or pipe clamps.

C-Clamps

C-clamps derive their name from the basic C shape of their steel or iron frames. One end of the C—the anvil—is fixed; it doesn't move at all. The other end is fitted with a threaded rod and swivel pad. When the threaded end is tightened, whatever is between it and the fixed end is tightly gripped. C-clamps come in a variety of styles and sizes, but they're generally small; woodworking C-clamps are usually limited to a 12" jaw opening. For the projects in this book, the 6" sizes will suffice.

C-clamps can't span great distances (a bar or pipe clamp serves that purpose), but they're ideal for holding narrow pieces of stock together and for clamping work near the edge of the bench. Deep-throated C-clamps allow you to apply pressure to the work piece at some distance from its edge.

Bar Clamps and Pipe Clamps

These clamps are made to span long or wide pieces of wood or to grip several pieces of wood that are placed edge-to-edge. (You'll find them useful, for instance, when gluing together the components of the Traditional Cutting Board or the Butcher Block Table.) Their frames are simply steel or aluminum bars or sections of iron plumbing pipe that are several feet in length. At one end is a fixed head, equipped with a short, threaded rod and a metal pad. At the other end is a sliding tail-stop that can be locked in any position along the bar or pipe to accommodate the work.

Pipe clamps are less expensive than (but not quite as effective as) bar clamps. If you need to keep expenses to a minimum, buy pipe-clamp kits, which include only the fixtures; you can purchase the pipe itself—and have its ends threaded—at a plumbing supply store. For our projects, six 30"-long, 3/4" pipe clamps will serve you well.

Vise

A vise is just a bench-mounted clamp. It can be used to hold work pieces together or to hold stock securely while you work on it. A woodworker's vise has smooth, broad jaws; these are usually drilled so that facings can be installed to prevent marring fine work. Better wood vises include a dog; this is a bar that slides up from the vise's movable jaw to hold work against a similar stop mounted on the bench itself. The dog extends the vise's effective jaw opening considerably. Some vises also make use of a half-nut to provide quick-slide opening and closing; tightening only occurs once the work is in place.

HOW TO USE CLAMPS

You'll use your clamps for one purpose that we haven't mentioned yet: dry-fitting. This process works just as it sounds. After components are cut, they're clamped together—without glue—to see if they fit properly. If they don't, you'll need to trim them here and there to remove high spots or long ends. Don't use a lot of pressure when you dry-fit your work; exerting too much force can split a joint or damage the wood.

Even though the construction procedures that we've written for each project don't often include a dry-fitting step, it's always wise to dry-fit the pieces you've cut before you fasten them together permanently.

Bar or pipe clamps are most appropriate for oversize clamping jobs because they can stretch to match the width or height of a project and still offer a secure grip. They're especially useful when you need to edge-glue pieces to make a wide board.

For joints or components less than 12" in depth, a C-clamp is the universal tool of choice. To keep its metal from marring your work, cut some 2"-square pads from scrap pieces of 1/4" plywood, and insert them between the clamp's pads and your work piece.

For angled components, where a bar or pipe clamp alone would have a difficult time getting a good purchase, you can make one work by C-clamping a temporary wooden wedge to an angled face so that the wedge's flat face is parallel to another wood face elsewhere on the project. The flat part of the wedge is then used as a platform to support the bar or pipe clamp's pad.

The best results in joint-clamping come when you place the clamp's pressure points directly at the center line of the work or joint to be glued. Snug-tightening is best; over-tightening can damage the wood or force enough glue from the joint to cause uneven distribution, thus weakening the joint.

With some projects (the One-Step Stool, for instance), you'll need to pre-drill "blind" holes through the face of one board and into the edge of a loose piece behind it. If that piece behind is too large or deep to be effectively clamped, you can create a temporary groove to hold it in place by clamping spaced 2 x 4 blocks to the back of the piece through which you'll be drilling. Slip the large piece into the groove created by the clamped blocks, and hold it by hand while you drill holes through the face of the piece in front.

MEASURING AND MARKING

Correctly measured and marked dimensions are your foundations for success, so don't underestimate the importance of your measuring and marking tools.

Measuring tools establish length, width, and depth. They're useful when you purchase raw stock (it's always wise to check the actual dimensions of lumber before you buy it), and they're absolutely necessary when you're constructing your project. Marking tools are helpful in locating the lines, points, curves, and angles where you intend to cut, rout, or bore.

If you'll be using more than a single measuring tool on a project (a tape measure and a straightedge, for instance), check the graduations on one tool against those on the other. The marked graduations on even the finest measuring tools will sometimes vary, and although these variations will be slight, knowing that they exist will allow you to compensate.

Steel Tape Measure

Steel tapes are just rulers that roll up. They're made in widths between 1/4" and 1" and in lengths from 6' to 25'. The tape end has a hook that secures to one end of the work; this should be loosely mounted to compensate for the width of the hook in both inside and outside measurements.

Graduations on a steel tape measure are noted in 1/16" increments (except for the first 12", which are marked in 1/32" increments). For our projects, a 3/4"-wide, 12'-long, self-retracting rule with a tape-lock button would be your best choice.

Straightedge

A straightedge comes in handy for close measuring work and for drawing straight lines. It's a steel ruler, 12" to 36" long, which can be used for both measuring and marking.

Try Square

This small (5-1/2" x 8") square is used to check right angles; it consists of a handle and a metal blade, set at a 90° angle to one another. A ruler along the edge of the blade can be used to take quick measurements.

Framing Square

A framing square is shaped like a large right angle and is used to check for 90° accuracy on a large scale. Its two edges are 16" and 24" long and are marked with ruler graduations in 1/8" and 1/16" increments.

Compass and Dividers

A divider has a pivot at the top and two legs, each with a pointed end. A compass is similar, but a pencil tip replaces one pointed end. These tools are used to scribe and transfer arcs, circles, and patterns during layout.

Utility Knife

This inexpensive tool can be used both to cut lines and to scribe them. The best versions have retractable blades and a blade storage pocket in the handle.

HOW TO MEASURE AND MARK

The careful carpenter's slogan, "measure twice, cut once," is overused (we've yet to read a woodworking book in which it doesn't appear), but the warning it offers never gets any less appropriate. We'd like to add one additional warning: No matter how many times you recheck your measurements, if you use the wrong measuring tool, you can still come up short.

The steel tape rule is often regarded as the backbone of the measuring business. Everyday measuring jobs fall to this tool because it's both fast and accurate (within 1/16"). Don't rely on a steel tape to strike a straight line, however, particularly over any distance. The metal band will lift or move no matter how careful you are, and it will literally throw you a curve. When you need to measure distances less than 36", a straightedge is your best bet; that's why we've recommended it for nearly every project in this book.

If the distance you need to mark is longer than your straightedge, use the tape to mark 2'-long increments, and then strike lines with the straightedge. When marking measured points, a V-shaped pencil mark works best, since the point of the V will show you right where to cut.

Establishing a square or perpendicular edge is the try square's job, one that must be completed every time you make a crosscut or transfer a line to the remaining three sides of a board. Use a try square on smaller pieces and a framing square on the larger ones. Rest the handle or head of the tool against the edge of the work, and use the blade as a ruler as you mark a line. To transfer that line to the other surfaces, simply "walk" the square around the work, using the tail of the previous line as the start of the next one.

To lay out the radius of a quarter- or half-circle, use the compass. Open the tool's legs to the desired radius, then place its point at the center of the partial circle you wish to make; swing the other leg to make the mark.

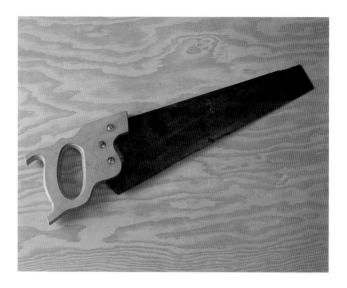

CUTTING

A saw's function is determined by the number, pitch, bevel, and angle of teeth on its blade. A saw with a high number of teeth per inch (a measurement known as points) won't cut quickly, but it will cut smoothly. A backsaw, for example, has 15 teeth per inch; it cuts slowly and is used for fine joinery work. A saw with fewer points will make a coarser cut, but it will also cut more rapidly. A crosscut saw, with perhaps 8 teeth per inch, can cut quickly across thick lumber.

Though most of the projects in this book could be made with hand tools, your cutting will probably be done with power saws and will certainly be easier if you use them. Power saws often use what are known as combination blades; these offer clean cuts both with and against the wood's grain.

Crosscut Saw

As its name suggests, this handsaw is used to cut across or against the wood's grain. Though crosscut saw lengths vary, a 26" one will work well for any handsawing that you do as you construct these projects. Crosscut saws are available with 7 through 12 points per inch, depending on how coarse or fine you wish the cut to be. Remember, the greater the number of points, the smoother the cut—and the more slowly it's made.

Ripsaw

A ripsaw is designed to cut with or along the wood's grain. Most ripsaws are 26" long and come with 4-1/2 through 7 points per inch. If you have no power saws, you'll want to own both a ripsaw and a crosscut saw; while it's possible to rip with a crosscut saw, you can't make a successful crosscut with a ripsaw.

Backsaw and Miter Box

A backsaw is smaller than either a ripcut or crosscut saw. The typical backsaw has a 12" blade with about 15 teeth per inch and is suitable for fine cutting. Its back consists of a stiff brass or steel spine, which keeps the blade from bending but which limits the depth of cut. This limitation isn't a concern for most joint-making.

A miter box is basically a saw guide and can be used with a backsaw to cut miters and bevels. The least expensive ones are simply U-shaped, open-ended boxes with fixed 45° and 90° saw-slots in them. The work piece is placed in the box, and the saw is guided by the angled grooves. Higher quality boxes come with saws that fit in a special jig and can be adjusted to cut at any angle up to 45° to the right and left of perpendicular.

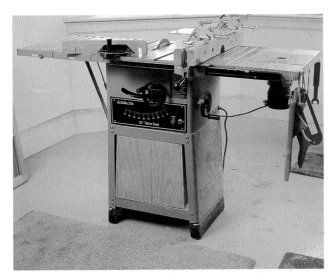

Coping Saw

The steel-bow frame of a coping saw is U-shaped. A very thin blade, with 10 to 12 teeth per inch, is mounted between the tips of the U. This saw is especially useful for cutting curves because its frame can be angled away from the line of cut. It won't do well on boards thicker than 3/4", however.

Circular Saw

The motor-driven, hand-held circular saw may be the most popular power tool in existence. The typical version has a 7-1/4" blade which can be adjusted to cut at 90°, 45°, and at any position in between. When set to cut at a perpendicular, blade penetration is 2-1/4"; at 45°, it's reduced to 1-3/4". A circular saw's greatest disadvantages are that it's heavy and can be cumbersome.

Better-quality circular saws are usually equipped with a carbide-tipped combination blade, but regular blades will do just as well if you replace them frequently.

Table Saw and Dado Blade

Unlike the circular saw, a table saw is not hand-held; it's built into a frame and table. Its weight and design will give you a more accurate cut than a hand-held circular saw can deliver, though it won't handle very thick boards. The typical version has a pivoting carriage that holds the blade's arbor, or axle. This carriage construction allows the blade to be raised to a 90° cutting depth of 3-1/8"—and tilted up to 45° (the cut at that angle is 2-1/8" deep).

Generally, table saws are equipped with a 10" carbide-tipped combination blade and have a more powerful motor than the hand-held variety. Compact and portable table saws with the same features as larger models, but that use smaller blades, are also available.

Table saws come with a rip fence; this is a long, straight piece that runs parallel to the exposed blade and that can be adjusted to either side of it. The fence assures accurate rip cuts by guiding material into the blade.

A miter gauge, which is adjustable to 45° on either side of a perpendicular midpoint, aids in making miter cuts by holding the stock at the correct angle as it's passed through the blade.

As we've mentioned before, you should leave the blade guard in place while you operate the tool; all modern table saws are equipped with one. The guard blocks flying wood chips and helps to prevent blade "kickback," which can cause serious injury.

A dado blade is a specially designed cutting tool that is fitted to a table saw to make wide grooves and notches. There are two common dado designs. One uses an offset blade that wobbles to the right and to the left as it revolves. The other design uses two outer blades and a number of inner chippers that are stacked to establish the width of the cut.

Jig and Sabre Saws

The hand-held jig or sabre saw is the power-driven alternative to a coping saw and is used to cut curves, shapes, and large holes in panels or boards up to 1-1/2" in thickness. Cutting action is provided by a narrow, reciprocating "bayonet" blade that moves very rapidly. A shoe surrounding the blade can be tilted 45° to the right and left of perpendicular for angled cuts.

The best jigsaws have a variable speed control and an orbital blade action; this action swings the cutting edge forward into the work and back again, through the blade's up-and-down cycle. A dust blower keeps the cut clear, and the tool may also come with a circle-cutting guide and rip fence as well.

Band Saw

A band saw isn't necessary for any of the projects in this book, but in spite of its cost, its ability to cut curves and circles—as well as stock over 3" thick—makes it a tool well worth owning if you spend a lot of time working with wood.

The saw is equipped with two (or sometimes three) wheels that guide a continuous band of steel blade within a fixed frame. The distance between the blade and frame is the throat depth; 10" or 12" is standard for most saws, with 3-wheel designs allowing considerably more clearance. Blades can be 1/8" to 3/4" wide and have—for wood cutting—from 4 to 12 teeth per inch.

The work is placed on a table, one that tilts to 45° from perpendicular for bevel cuts. A blade guide just above the work can be raised or lowered to suit the thickness of the stock being cut. A miter gauge helps in cutting bevels and angles.

HOW TO MAKE CUTS

The projects' Suggested Tools lists indicate which saw (or saws) you'll need once you've started the construction process, but they won't tell you which saws to use as you cut the original wood to size. If, after you've read this section, you're still unsure of which saw will work best as you cut your lumber to the dimensions called for in the Materials lists, you can either have the wood cut for you at your lumberyard or ask the salesperson there to tell you which saw will do the job best.

After you've done your measuring and marking, making the cuts is simply a matter of following the instructions that come with your saw and the ones provided with your project. Keep in mind that your personal safety—especially when using power tools—is a prime concern. Ask yourself what the consequences of each move will be before you make it! And keep alert; sometimes the drone of a blade or the sight of it spinning through the work can be dangerously hypnotic.

When you start a cut with a handsaw, grip the saw firmly—but not tensely—with the back of its handle squarely against the ball of your palm. Begin by placing the saw's teeth on the "waste" (or outer) side of your marked line, and draw the saw back toward you a few times, guiding the teeth with the outer edge of your thumb. Once the cut has been started, exert pressure only on the downstrokes, and keep the blade square with the surface of the wood. For crosscuts, hold the saw at a 45° angle; for rip cuts, hold it at 60°.

When you use a circular saw, make sure that the blade depth is set so that the saw's teeth penetrate the opposite face of the work fully; this way, the blade will be less likely to jam. Usually, the blade is set by loosening a knob or lever and moving the shoe. Make sure that your sawhorses or supports aren't in the blade's path, or you'll cut them as well as your work piece.

Find a comfortable stance before starting the saw. Don't grip the handle too tightly, or your tired hand may cause an inaccurate cut. Larger circular saws come with a second grip at the front for added control, but keep in mind that two-fisted sawing requires well-clamped work.

Before starting a cut, draw the power cord behind you. Always wear safety glasses, and sight your line of cut along the mark on the front of the saw's shoe. The safety guard will swing up by itself as you move forward. A combination blade with a circular saw will enable you to make a rip cut or a crosscut.

A table saw allows more precise cutting because it has a fence and a miter gauge. Set the cutting depth with the handwheel located at the front of the saw cabinet. The blade should penetrate the work deeply enough that several full teeth are exposed; this allows the sawdust to escape and the blade to cool.

To adjust the fence, loosen its lock and slide it to the right or left as needed. You can use the gauge on the fence rails to measure the width of cut, but a more accurate method is to take a steel tape reading between the fence's edge and the tip of a blade tooth. Pick a tooth that's set toward, not away from, the fence.

Allow the motor a few seconds to come up to speed after you start it; never shove a piece of wood into a slowly moving blade. And don't put your hands near the spinning blade; use a push stick to pass the work through. Why? A kickback or a quick stall can put your fingers right into the saw's teeth.

Curve-cutting isn't difficult if your cutting line is clearly marked. For thinner material and tight contours, use the thin-bladed coping saw; it's easily controlled. If your stock is more than 3/8" or so in thickness, or if the marked line is greater than the saw's throat depth, a jigsaw makes cutting easier and more accurate. The tighter the curve or circle, the thinner the jigsaw blade should be. Blades that are too thick can bind or overheat, warping the steel and affecting the straightness of the cutting slot (otherwise known as the saw kerf).

Cutting at an angle, as you do when you make miters and bevels, can be done in several ways. If the wood is less than 6" in width, a miter box makes the most accurate miter cut. Held freehand, a backsaw or a larger crosscut saw can do well if the cutting line is clearly marked.

A circular saw shoe can be adjusted to a 45° angle for bevel cutting. Similarly, the table saw's blade carriage can be pivoted to the same degree by using the handwheel on the side of the saw cabinet.

Rabbets and grooves can be cut with a table saw fitted with a dado blade, though with most projects it's easier to make these cuts with a router and a straight bit. To use the table saw for this purpose, remove the table insert, and set the dado head width; how you do this will depend upon the blade design. The offset "wobbler" type has a rotating hub that changes the width by altering the degree of offset. The stacked type must be set up out of the saw and then reinstalled on the arbor. When you stack the chippers between the outer blades, make sure that the teeth rest between the gullets of the adjacent blades and that the chippers are staggered around the circumference. Adjust the depth of the blade with the handwheel, and set the fence to establish the width of the rabbet as the work is passed through the saw.

Dadoes (like those in the Onion Bins) and grooves for splines and tongues are cut by running the edge of the frame piece through the blade after it's been adjusted for proper width and depth.

DRILLING

Boring holes through wood requires the use of drills and bits suited for the job. Holes can be purely decorative or designed with special features such as a tapered countersink or an internal shoulder.

3/8" Variable Speed, Reversible Drill

Though you can bore almost any hole with a hand-operated drill, it's almost silly not to own this inexpensive and versatile tool, which operates more quickly and with less effort than any of its hand-operated relatives. For the projects in this book (and for many that you'll encounter elsewhere), a drill with a 3/8" chuck capacity and a motor amperage of 3.5 amps or greater will do just fine. Cordless versions are available and are appropriate for driving screws and drilling small holes, but they may not be suitable for continuous, heavy-duty work.

For a bit more money, you can get an electric drill with a variable speed control. This feature allows you to govern the speed of the drill's motor by varying the pressure you exert on the tool's trigger. A reversible motor is another inexpensive feature, one which will permit you to take screws out just as quickly as you insert them.

Depth Control Stop Collars

When you need to control the depth of a drill bit's penetration, use a stop collar. These are metal (or sometimes plastic) rings which lock onto the drill bit's shaft. When the bit sinks into the wood, the collar hits the wood's face and stops the bit from going any deeper. Stop collars are sized to fit different drill bit diameters.

Countersinks

Nothing is added to a project's appearance when the head of a screw protrudes above the face of the wood. In order to hide these heads, a countersink is used. These bits cut shallow, slope-sided holes into the surface of the work, creating a recess in which the screw's head can rest flush with the face of the work. A more versatile adaptation of the countersink (the pilot bit with countersink) is described in the next section.

Specialty Bits

A variety of drill bits are made to accomplish specific tasks. Forstner bits, for example, are used to drill crisp, flat-bottomed holes for fine joinery work. These bits are made in 1/4" to 2-1/4" diameters. Spade bits bore quickly and make moderately clean holes through wood. They're designed with a center point and two flat cutting edges, and come in 1/4" to 1-1/2" diameters. Bradpoint bits have a center point that prevents the bit

from "skating" across a surface and that leaves clean sides in the hole; standard sizes range from 1/8" to 1/2".

Pilot bits with countersinks (or counterbores) combine the hole-drilling and countersinking processes in one operation. The better versions of these bits use what's known as a tapered bit, which follows the contour of a standard wood screw; they also include a stop collar. These combination bits are made for screw sizes Nos. 5 through 12, and for most of the projects in this book, are usually used in conjunction with a stop collar. This type of drill bit is particularly versatile because it allows the woodworker to countersink a fastener flush with the wood's surface or counterbore the hole so that wood filler or a dowel plug can be used to cover the screw head completely.

Hole Saws

Hole saws, as you might guess, cut holes; they're really saws, not drill bits, but because they're powered by drills, we've included them in this section. They're drum-like cutters, equipped with a circular row of teeth at one end, and are mounted on the end of a drill shaft. These saws are available in 3/4" to 3" sizes and are generally used when the hole needed is too large to be handled by a standard drill with a specialty bit.

HOW TO DRILL HOLES

A wood screw hole consists of three parts: the pilot or lead hole (which is a little more than half the diameter of the screw itself), the shank hole (which is the same diameter as the screw), and the sink or bore (the hole in which the screw head is recessed to bring it below the surface of the wood).

In softwoods, it's not really necessary to drill more than the pilot hole. And to give the threads a better bite, the hole is sunk only a little more than half the length of the screw. In very dense hardwoods and when you use long screws, however, you may need to drill the shank hole too. Make that hole only as deep as the shank—the unthreaded portion of the screw—is long. Note that screws driven into wood's end-grain have less than half the holding power of a screw driven perpendicular to the grain.

Combination pilot bits with countersinks make hole-drilling a relatively simple task. They're sized by screw numbers, and their stop collars and countersinks are adjustable for length. Many have specially tapered bits that accommodate standard wood screws perfectly.

In softwoods, when you're using No. 6 or No. 8 diameter screws, self-tapping power-driven screws—sometimes called drywall screws—are even more convenient, though you should take care to pre-drill the pilot holes when driving screws near the end of the wood. These screws will work in hardwoods as well, but the screw holes must be pre-drilled at all times, or you may split the wood or shear the screw head off when you drive the fastener in place.

If the required diameters are small enough (1/4" or 3/8"), you can bore sockets for dowels with a regular drill bit. Larger holes require either a spade bit or—better yet—a Forstner bit; the latter produces a clean, flat-bottomed hole. When you don't trust yourself to gauge the depth of a socket accurately, use a stop collar on a standard drill bit.

Drill through-holes and bores with care if you want to avoid tearing out the back side of the work, especially when another piece is planned to face it. You can avoid splintering wood this way by first drilling part of the way through the piece and then inserting the drill bit from the hole's opposite side. If you use a small pilot bit, the hole it creates when it penetrates through to the back face will help you to locate the point at which to start the second bore.

CHISELING

A wide variety of chisels is available to woodworkers, but because the types of joinery used in our projects are fairly simple, you'll only need one type.

Cabinetmaker's Chisel

To clean up joints and to complete the general paring and shaving work required when you prepare to fit wood pieces together, you'll find that a standard 1/2" cabinetmaker's chisel proves useful. A set of four or five bevel-edge chisels for hand or light mallet work, in sizes from 1/4" to 1" wide and 9" to 11" long, is more than sufficient. For most of these projects, you'll probably be manipulating your chisel by hand instead of striking it with a hammer or mallet, but for future reference, be sure that your chisels' handles are reinforced if you intend to use a mallet, or they may split with use.

HOW TO USE A CHISEL

Surfaces that haven't been completely cut with a saw or router will need to be straightened and smoothed with a chisel. The job is an easy one as long as you maintain the chisel's sharp edge.

On most work, you won't need to use a mallet. Hold the chisel in your right hand to provide the driving effort, and control the blade's direction with your left. If you do use a mallet, strike the chisel handle lightly in order to avoid taking big bites at one time. Work with the grain, and hold the tool at a slight angle (right or left) whenever possible; this technique provides the smoothest cuts and is least likely to dull the blade. To avoid gouging the work, don't drive the edge too steeply. Instead, hold the blade level at a slight downward angle. The flat surface—not the beveled edge—of the chisel should face the wood you're cutting.

ROUTING

Cutting grooves and rabbets, shaping edges, and making slots are all jobs that a router can do easily and quickly. You'll find, for instance, that a number of our projects include decoratively rounded edges. These were cut with a router and roundover bit. You could

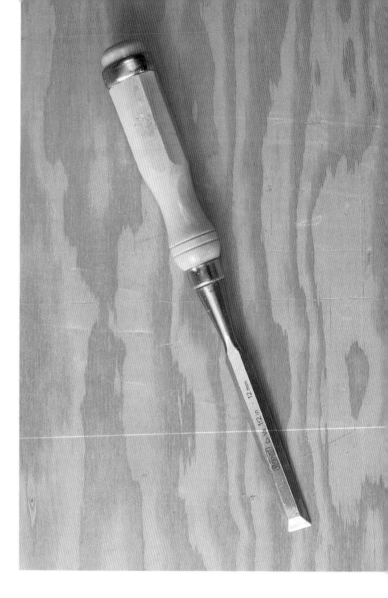

create similar edges with gouges, rasps, and sanders, but not without spending an awfully long time—and probably not without some visible irregularities in the design!

Router

The simplest routers have 3/8" collets, external clamp-depth controls, and 6-amp motors. More sophisticated models are known as plunge routers; these allow vertical entry into the work for precise cutting and have 1/2" collets, variable-speed 12- to 15-amp motors, and variable depth controls.

Routers hold bits in a collet on the end of a shaft, which in turn is supported by a flat base and housing. The shape of the bit determines what type of cut will be made in the work, and handles on the housing allow the operator to control the direction of the bit.

Router Bits

The design and shape of a router bit dictates what form the finished edge or groove will take. There are over two hundred router-bit styles available for various types of work, though for the projects in this book, only a half-dozen or so are needed. When cutting or shaping an edge, a router bit with a ball-bearing pilot at its tip is used. The tip rolls along the edge below the portion of the wood being trimmed, assuring a high degree of accuracy in the cut. Groove- or slot-cutting bits cannot use pilot tips, so when channels are routed, a guide or temporary fence is often used. Either type of bit can be set vertically by adjusting the router base to control the depth of cut.

Router Guide

A popular accessory for any size router is an edge guide. This device clamps onto the base of the tool and acts as a moving fence to keep the router and bit following an edge of the work. The guide is laterally adjustable to suit work of varying widths.

Router Table

A hand-held router works well when the piece you're shaping is large enough to clamp securely to a table and large enough to provide a steady base for the router itself. When the work piece is small or very narrow, however, it's much easier to move the work into the router rather than move the router into the work. To hold the router stationary, a router table is used. This is simply a flat surface with a hole cut into it. The router is turned upside down and fastened to the underside of

the surface so that the router bit protrudes up and through the hole. The work piece is then eased across the surface and into the moving bit.

HOW TO USE A ROUTER

The router accomplishes more quickly and cleanly what would normally be the tedious process of using a saw, a gouge, a file, and a chisel. If you were to build every project in this book, you'd need eight router bits: 1/4" and 1/2" straight bits, 1/4" and 3/8" roundover bits, a 45° 7/16" chamfer bit, a 3/8" cove bit, a 5/32" ogee bit, and a 1/4" core box bit. The shape of the router bits' cutting surfaces determine what the finished edge or groove will look like. A chamfer bit, for example, makes a 45° bevel on the face of what was a square edge; likewise, a core box bit cuts a clean, rounded groove into a flat surface.

When you operate a router, grasp it comfortably in both hands, and position yourself so that you have a clear view of the working bit (eye protection is a must!). Move the router from left to right; if circular or irregular cutting is required, then the motion should be counter-clockwise. To avoid chipping, make any cuts across the end grain of your work first; then rout with the grain. By loosening the router's base and then adjusting the motor housing, you can control the depth of cut.

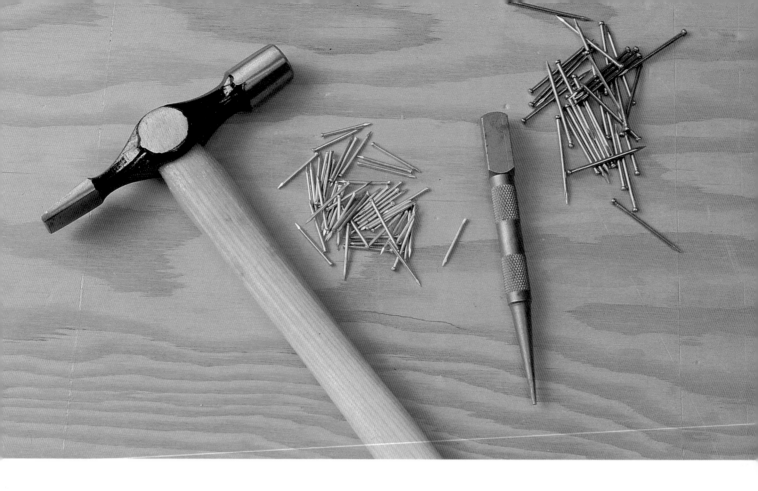

Before making any permanent cuts, we highly recommend that you run a test on a piece of scrap wood to see what your work will look like, especially if you haven't had much experience with router work. Practice will improve your control of the tool. After a while, you'll be able to rely on the depth gauge marked on the router's side instead of having to test-cut.

Freehand work is fine for short jobs or when the bit is equipped with a pilot bearing, but when you're cutting long dadoes and grooves, you'll probably need to clamp the wood to a bench and use the tool's base-mounted straight guide to keep the cut consistent. If you don't have a guide, you can often create a substitute by clamping a straight section of 1 x 2 to the bench or work, alongside and parallel to the line of cut.

When you're edge-rabbeting grooves like those in the Cork Board project, place a piece of scrap stock to the right and left of the work, flush with the working surface. This will prevent the router base from tilting to one side and spoiling the cut. It will also give you a place to mount a guide, if you use one.

FASTENING

Though a beginning woodworker might challenge what we're about to say, none of the projects in this book are complex! What makes them comparatively simple is their joinery—the way one piece is fastened to another. (You won't need to make a single mortise-and-tenon or dovetail joint.) We've tried to include only the simplest and most widely available of fasteners, and we've minimized the kind and number of tools you'll need to put your projects together.

Hammer and Nail Set

The only hammer you're likely to need for these projects is a lightweight tack hammer, 3-1/2 or 6 ounces in weight at most. A claw style will do, but what's known as a Warrington hammer is best because as well as having one traditional flat face, it also has one elongated peen for starting small brads.

Should you need a larger hammer for chisel work or for setting joints, an 8" wooden carpenter's mallet (12 ounces or so in weight) will do well. Plastic-headed mallets are also useful for this type of work.

A nail set is simply a fine-pointed punch. It's used to set the head of a finishing nail or brad below the wood's surface without enlarging the nail hole.

Screwdrivers

The screw fasteners called for in our projects take a No. 2 Phillips head screwdriver. A 6" or 8" one, with a molded or wooden handle, will work well on both No. 6 and No. 8 screws.

A 3/16" flat-bladed screwdriver, 6" or 8" in length, can be used if you only have access to straight-slotted screws. It can also serve as a small pry bar to open eye-rings and to turn screw eyes.

These days, most woodworkers use power-drive bits in combination with drywall screws (sharp-pointed wood screws) to speed up the monotonous job of screw-sinking. These bits—used with 3/8" variable-speed power drills—have a short, six-sided shank which slips easily into the drill chuck. The tip can be a Phillips or straight-bladed design, though a square-drive tip (to fit matching screws) is becoming more popular with time.

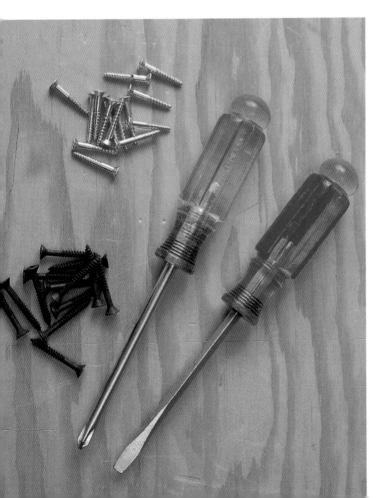

Screws and Nails

For the sake of convenience, we've only used a few types of fasteners for these projects. No. 8 flathead Phillips screws, 1" and 1-1/4" in length, are called for in many projects. No. 6 flathead Phillips screws—for the most part brass—are used when flush-mounting the fasteners will enhance the project's appearance.

A standard flathead wood screw holds joints and components very well. But the modern drywall, or sharp-point woodworking screw, is an improvement on the old standard because it's designed to be used with a power driver. Power-driven screws for woodworking are either the cross-slotted Phillips style or the newer square-drive type.

Brads (wire nails) serve for narrow joints and trim. The 16-gauge x 1-1/4" brad is used to secure mitered joints and recessed dowel joints. The thinner 18-gauge x 3/4" brad is more suitable for securing thin strips and trim pieces.

Glues and Adhesives

We've recommended two types of wood glues for these projects. For general gluing, where exposure to moisture would be minimal or nonexistent, a common yellow carpenter's glue (or aliphatic resin) will work well. It sets in about ten minutes, cures in 12 to 24 hours, and can be thinned with water to promote penetration into the wood grain for a stronger joint.

For gluing cutting boards or other pieces that will probably be exposed to water, a non-toxic waterproof wood glue is more appropriate. The pre-catalyzed aliphatic resin now on the market offers the same advantages as the yellow carpenter's glue, but it resists the effects of water and weather. If this type of adhesive isn't available, you may use the more costly two-part resorcinol, though it takes about 12 hours to set and at least another 12 to cure completely.

No matter which glue you use, if any runs from a joint, wipe it from the surface of the wood with a damp cloth, or it will make the wood difficult to sand and finish. The amber-colored stain of dried glue will show through many finishes.

Tiles (such as those used in the Tiled Trivets project) are fastened most effectively with a powder-based latex cement adhesive, one that's waterproof and heat-resistant. Old-fashioned mastics and many household-grade liquid cements may not be able to withstand the heat of a trivet in use.

HOW TO HOLD THINGS TOGETHER

When you're drilling the pilot holes for the screw fasteners in these projects, you'll need to set the stop collar for the correct depth. The depth set-up for every screw in all 50 projects is clearly indicated in the construction procedures. We've taken into account the counterbore needed for plugging the screw holes (if the heads aren't flush-mounted), and we've allowed some buffer beyond the point of the screw on joints and surfaces that are exposed.

One word of caution: Softwoods have a tendency to give, and power drivers can sink a screw farther and faster than you might think. Avoid driving a screw point through the back surface of exposed joints—we guarantee that it will ruin your project's appearance!

Especially when you're working with hardwoods, don't insert fasteners too tightly, or you'll strip screw heads or split the joints. Joints often tighten over time, anyway; wood swells slightly as it absorbs indigenous moisture.

When brads are called for, you can avoid splitting the wood by using a small-diameter drill bit to pre-drill holes for them. Pre-drilled holes are especially important when you're driving brads close to the end of the wood or in mitered joints. We've recommended a tack hammer for driving brads because of the control it offers. If you use a larger hammer (in the 12- to 16-ounce range), be careful not to bend the wire body of the brad or send it home at an extreme angle. And with any hammer, don't miss your mark, or you'll mar the wood.

When you set a brad beneath the wood's surface, use the smallest nail set practical. Drive the head of the brad just below the wood's surface—not too deeply. The hole will be easier to fill if it remains shallow.

To give glue the best opportunity to work, make sure that the surfaces to be joined are dry, and that they're free of loose material and surface oils. They should also meet flush to each other because aliphatic resins are not intended to fill gaps. You can strengthen joints by diluting the yellow woodworkers' glue that we've recommended with water; this will allow the resins to soak deeply into the wood's grain. Don't forget to wipe up any drips or drops as soon as you see them!

Aliphatic resins set up in about ten minutes and are fully cured in 24 hours. Coat both wood surfaces with a liberal application of glue, and then clamp the pieces together. Remember not to over-tighten the clamps; doing so can force so much glue from the joint that there's not enough left on the wood to do the job.

The latex cement adhesive that you'll use to glue tiles in place comes in powder form. Mix it with water to the consistency of toothpaste (don't make it too liquid), and butter the back of the tile and the wooden bed, using a putty knife or a small trowel. Press the tile down, and wiggle it in place to seat it. If you spread the cement evenly, it will fill the gap around the tile's edges, thereby acting as a grout. Wipe off any excess cement with a damp cloth.

PLUGGING AND FILLING

Screw heads that are counterbored—set below the surface of the wood—are usually covered in some way to improve the appearance of the project.

Dowel Plugs

A 1/4"-deep socket above the screw head allows plenty of room for a dowel plug, a short piece of doweling that is glued in place and then sanded down flush to the wood's surface. Once it's smoothed off, the plug can be stained to match the background species or left to contrast with the wood around it. In some projects (the Butcher Block Table, for example), you'll use what's known as a roundtop plug; this type of plug protrudes above the surface.

Wood Filler

Bores shallower than 1/4" can accept a plug, but they usually get covered with a wood filler. Fillers aren't as durable as plugs in larger holes because they can shrink and crack. To cover nail holes, however, they're ideal. When choosing a wood filler, be aware that some can't take a stain, and others can't be used under urethane topcoats. Read the label carefully before you make your purchase.

Putty Knife

When you need to fill defects or fastener holes in wood with wood filler, a flexible putty knife with a 1-1/4"-broad blade works best. Use one corner of the blade to pack filler into the hole; then use the blade's flat edge to smooth the surface of the work even with the surrounding wood. Your putty knife will also prove handy when you lay adhesive cement for tiles.

SMOOTHING AND SANDING

To properly finish a piece of wood, it's often necessary to level surfaces (by removing excess material) and to make the grain smooth. Hand-held bench planes do the hard work when it's needed; files and rasps cut for detail and in small areas; sandpaper prepares the wood for its final finish.

Rasps and Files

Wood rasps are coarse-cutting tools used to make the first cut in removing wood stock for shaping or rounding. A finer cabinet rasp is made for second-cut work. Rasps come in three styles: flat on both sides, half-round on one side, and round.

Wood files are less coarse than rasps and are used for finer smoothing and finishing work. They usually come in round and half-round cross sections; like rasps, they're about 10" long.

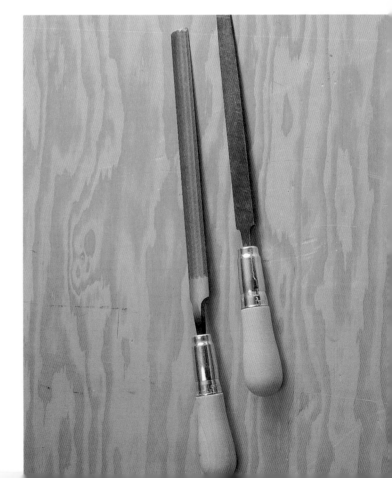

For the projects in this book, only two files are necessary: a half-round bastard file and a smooth file. A bastard-cut file is one step finer than a coarse file. The half-round back on this 10" or 12" tool allows it to be used on inside curves and arcs. For finish work, the smooth-cut file is best because it's the least coarse of the group and is especially useful in preparing hard-woods for sanding work.

Sanders and Sandpaper

Sanding can be done by hand or with power sanders. If you choose to sand by hand, you'll want to purchase a hand-sanding block. This is a small, palm-held, hard rubber tool with a flat surface at the bottom and some type of clip mechanism at each end to keep the sand-paper tightly in place.

Two types of power sanders are suitable for our pro-jects. The orbital finishing sander is hand-held; the most comfortable varieties have a palm grip and either a round or square pad to which sandpaper is attached. The orbit-

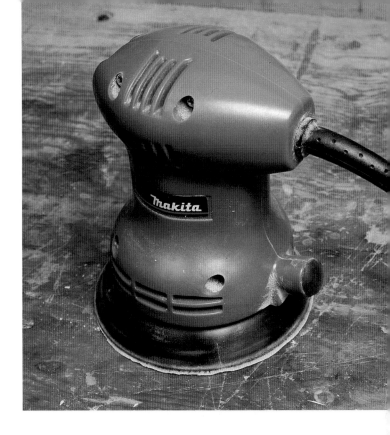

ing mechanism requires a 1-1/2- or 2-amp motor to be effective. For convenience, the round styles use self-adhesive paper on the pad rather than mechanical clips.

A belt sander, also hand-held, is a much more powerful tool. In fact, if you've never used one before, you'll definitely need to practice before using one on a project. The tool is held in both hands and moved from one end of the work piece to the other while its power-driven belt rotates. If you don't have access to a power sander, don't worry—just plan on spending extra time. You'll do what pre-power carpenters did—rely on patience and a hand-held sander instead.

Sandpaper and the replaceable belts for belt sanders come in a variety of grits (or degrees of roughness): coarse (No. 60), medium (No. 100), fine (No. 150), and extra-fine (No. 220). Other grits in between are also manufactured. Standard garnet paper is suitable for woodworking and is unique in that its abrasive particles continuously break away, exposing fresh material as they do. Aluminum-oxide sanding sheets, however, are more durable and less likely to clog.

FINISHING

A finish protects the wood but still allows it to adjust to the humidity and temperature of its environment. In this section, we'll go over the several finishes that we've recommended. Note that because we've chosen wood species that enhance each project's appearance, you won't find any information on stains. If you don't like our choices of wood species or if their colors don't complement your kitchen decor, feel free to wipe on a stain before applying a top-coat finish.

Lacquer

On projects that need moderate protection—those which won't be knocked around or stepped on—a lacquer coating is our recommended choice. Lacquer is resistant to moisture, heat, and alcohol, and it dries to a clear, relatively hard finish. In years gone by, brushed lacquer applications were tedious and time-consuming. These days, spray lacquer is available; the finish is spread in a fine, self-leveling coat and takes very little time or talent to apply. Sprays are available in individual 10- or 16-ounce cans, or (for use with airbrush or sprayer equipment) by the quart or gallon.

Polyurethane

On projects that are likely to encounter rougher use, such as the One-Step Stool, we've recommended a spray polyurethane finish. Urethane-based top coatings are even more resistant to abrasion than lacquers. A gloss finish is the hardest, but if you prefer the appearance of a satin finish, go ahead and use one.

Most polyurethanes are meant for indoor use, since the sun's ultraviolet (UV) rays affect the finish's composition even after it has dried. If any of your projects will be exposed to direct sunlight, check the product label to make sure that the polyurethane you choose is acceptable for exterior use.

Individually packaged spray polyurethane can be almost twice as expensive as the equivalent lacquer; if you're trying to hold down costs, buy polyurethane by the pint or quart and brush it on. If you do buy the brush-on variety, purchase a high-quality 1-1/2" synthetic brush, and spread the coating according to the instructions on the label. Don't shake the can before using the polyurethane, or you'll trap air bubbles in the mix. Instead, stir it gently with a clean paint paddle.

Food-Grade Bowl Finish

Items that will come in contact with food, like the cutting boards and some of the racks, need a non-toxic finish, so when we've used an oil finish, we've suggested a non-spoiling formula, food-grade, bowl finish. Please don't use tung oil on eating utensils; it's mildly toxic. And avoid salad oils, which provide a feast for bacteria and grow rancid with time! You'll find a number of salad-bowl oils and finishes that are perfect for these projects right at your hardware or building supply store.

HOW TO APPLY FINISHES

Be sure to work in a well-ventilated area when you work with either lacquer or polyurethane; their vapors can be dangerous to your health. Read the application instructions on the label thoroughly; they'll provide the best possible advice for application.

Both lacquer and polyurethane finishes are available with reduced Volatile Organic Compounds (VOCs), the irritating vapors that are released at room temperatures. Some manufacturers specifically market these reduced-

VOC products for health-conscious individuals, and they're available if you take the time to search for them.

Apply an oil finish with a clean cloth or work the oil into the wood with your fingers. The warmth of your fingers will help the grain to absorb the oils. Give the wood as many applications as are recommended on the label instructions, and be sure to allow adequate time for the project to dry before you put it to use.

WALL-MOUNTING

Some of the projects in this book are meant to be fastened to the wall or hung from the ceiling. Because house and kitchen construction varies, we haven't indicated how to space the project's mounting holes. Instead, this section provides some rules of thumb for attaching your racks and shelves.

Many of you will be mounting your finished work to what's known as drywall or sheetrock. This is the 5/8" hardened gypsum skin that covers the wooden framing members in the walls of your house. Drywall is fine for hanging pictures, but a project that's quite heavy should be mounted to the wood behind the drywall's surface, not just to the drywall itself.

In a properly constructed house, the vertical framing members, (or studs), are set every 16" or 24", depending upon how much weight the wall supports. One way to locate a stud within the wall is to bang on the drywall surface, and mark the points where the hollow sound stops and the solid sound begins. Another is to look closely for evidence of drywall nails; if you see bumps or patches on the wall, in vertical rows, a stud is probably standing behind them. If these two methods don't work, magnetic and electronic stud-finders (available at home improvement centers) will more accurately locate the studs for you.

Ideally, the projects should be mounted with two No. 6 x 2-1/4" flathead wood or drywall screws. Pre-drill the holes in the project using a countersink bit, with the stop collar set so that the head of the screw is just flush with the surface of the wood. (Use brass screws if you prefer a more finished look.) Space these holes to match the center-to-center distance between the studs. On projects narrower than 16", center the project over a single stud, and use one screw in the center and one in line below it.

If it isn't practical to mount your project to two studs, or to one stud with two screws, you can secure the project by fastening it with one wood-mounted screw (driven into the stud) and two drywall-mounted screws held in place with expansion anchors—better know as "molly" bolts. This type of anchor is inserted through a 1/4" hole drilled into the drywall. As the screw is tightened, the anchor draws up and expands to catch the back of the wall board. Expansion anchors come with their own screws; wood or drywall screws aren't meant to fit them. A variation of the molly bolt, known as the self-drilling anchor, is installed using a No. 2 Phillips screwdriver. This type of drywall anchor works with almost any type of screw.

If your home is older and has plaster walls, the same principles apply, except that you should use 1/8" toggle bolt anchors, which need a 3/8" hole drilled through the wall at each mounting point. These anchors also use their own screws. A newer-style, self-drilling toggle bolt can also be used; it's installed with a Phillips screwdriver and comes with its own hardware.

If your walls are faced with tongue-and-groove paneling or wainscot strips more than 3/8" thick, you can fasten No. 6 screws directly to the wood. Use molly bolts to support any weight when your walls are covered with thinner sheet paneling.

MOVING ON

One reminder before you move on to the projects themselves: Practice! Not even the finest of tools or most advanced of techniques can compensate for lack of experience, so take the time to scrounge for some scrap wood at lumberyards and specialty-wood suppliers. Then clamp, measure, mark, cut, drill, chisel, rout, smooth, and fasten until you feel really comfortable with the tools and techniques you'll be using.

...remove the cover and add in a thin steady stream. As
...the oil is added turn off the motor. Chill the dressing.

...onnaise
...e grated rind of 1/2 lemon and salt to taste. Just before
...grated horseradish.

...1/3 cup tomato purée, the juice of 1 lemon, 1 teaspoon
...and pepper to taste.

...onnaise
... cup Roquefort or bleu cheese, pressed through a fine
... a few drops of Tabasco sauce.

... I
... 5 tablespoons chili sauce, 2 teaspoons each of pimiento
...nd 1 tablespoon lime juice.

... II
... tablespoons caviar, 1 tablespoon finely chopped onion,
...ire sauce, and 1/2 teaspoon dry mustard. Let the dressing
...ng.

Mayonnaise

The Projects

A Box for Wooden Utensils

When your kitchen drawers begin to make you look like a shoplifter without a resale outlet, it's time to shift some of those utensils to an accessible counter top. This handy box will hold a surprising number of utensils and can be placed almost anywhere—next to a stove, in a corner by the area where you do most of your food preparation, or on a sunny windowsill.

Materials List

Cypress is recommended for this project.

(2) 3/8" x 3-1/2" x 6"   Sides
(2) 3/8" x 2-3/4" x 6"   Sides
(1) 3/8" x 2-3/4" x 2-3/4"   Bottom

Suggested Tools

Router
5/32" ogee bit
Tack hammer
Nail set
Putty knife
36" straightedge

Hardware & Supplies

Yellow wood glue
18-gauge x 3/4" brads
Wood filler
Spray lacquer

Construction Procedure

1. Apply a small amount of glue to one long edge of a 2-3/4" side piece.

2. Nail a 3-1/2" side piece to it, so that the 3-1/2" piece's edge is flush with the outer face of the 2-1/2" piece. Space the brads 3/16" from the edge so that they don't interfere with the router work later.

3. Apply glue to one long edge of the second 2-3/4" side piece. Then nail the first 3-1/2" piece to it.

4. Glue the exposed edges of the two 2-3/4" pieces to the remaining 3-1/2" side piece. Nail the last side piece in place.

5. Next, glue the edges of the 2-3/4" x 2-3/4" bottom piece, and carefully insert it into the space created by the four sides. Place one brad in each side of the box to secure the bottom.

6. With a nail set, sink all the brads. Fill the holes with wood filler.

7. When the glue has dried, rout the four long edges and the eight top and bottom edges, using a 5/32" ogee bit in the router. Set the bit no deeper than 1/8".

8. Sand the box lightly, and finish with several coats of spray lacquer.

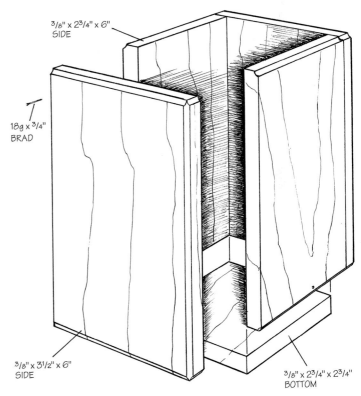

Traditional Cutting Board

Traditional, solid, attractive, and necessary—the cutting board is any kitchen's most dependable accessory. It protects your knives' blades from premature dulling, it defends your counters from scratches, and it can do double-duty as a tray when you're moving what you've sliced from the counter to the stove. This board's classic design is simple to construct, and with a little care, the finished project will last for years.

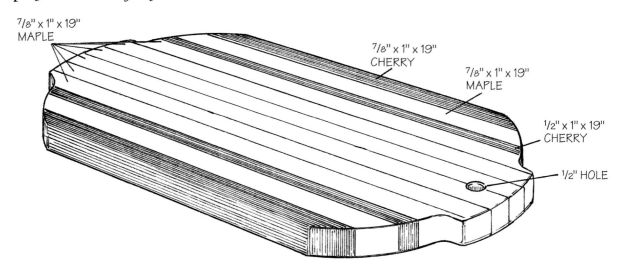

7/8" x 1" x 19" MAPLE

7/8" x 1" x 19" CHERRY

7/8" x 1" x 19" MAPLE

1/2" x 1" x 19" CHERRY

1/2" HOLE

Materials List

Maple and Cherry are recommended for this
project.

(8) 7/8" x 1" x 19"   Maple strips
(2) 7/8" x 1" x 19"   Cherry strips
(2) 1/2" x 1" x 19"   Cherry strips

Suggested Tools

Router
3/8" roundover bit
1/4" roundover bit
3/8" drill
1/2" drill bit
Pipe clamps
Jigsaw
Sander
Try square
36" straightedge

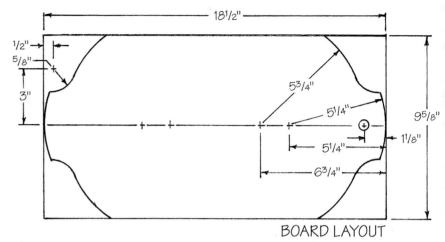

BOARD LAYOUT

Hardware & Supplies

Waterproof wood glue
Food-grade bowl finish

Construction Procedure

1. Lay out the strips so that their 1" dimensions
comprise the cutting board's thickness. On each side, a
7/8"-wide maple piece is bordered by a 1/2" cherry strip
to the inside and a 7/8" cherry strip on the outside. The
center is made up of six 7/8"-wide maple strips.

2. Spread glue evenly on all the edges to be joined,
and clamp the pieces in place evenly and squarely. Let
the assembly dry overnight. Sand the surfaces flat once
the glue has set.

3. Trim the piece to 9-5/8" x 18-1/2" dimensions.

4. Measure across the board's width to locate its
center, and strike a center line down the length of the
board.

5. Measure 5-1/4" in from each end, and mark
on the line. Using these marks as pivot points, draw a
5-1/4" radius at each end of the board with your compass (see Board Layout).

6. Then measure 6-3/4" in from each end, and mark
at the center line. Using the 6-3/4" marks as pivot points
for your compass, strike a 5-3/4" radius at each end.

7. Measure 3" to each side of the center line at
both ends of the board, and strike lines along the length
of the board.

8. On each of these lines and at both ends of the
board, measure and mark a point 1/2" in from the
board's edge.

9. Strike a 5/8" radius from each of these four
points; it will intersect with the 5-1/4" and 5-3/4" radii.

10. On one end, measure in 1-1/8", and drill a 1/2"
hole at the center line.

11. With a jigsaw, cut the marked outline of the
board. Sand the board smooth.

12. Using the 3/8" roundover bit, rout all the
board's edges.

13. Change over to a 1/4" roundover bit, and rout
both sides of the 1/2" hole.

14. Sand the board and hole lightly, and finish the
wood with several coats of a food-grade bowl finish.

Over-the-Sink Cutting Board

The single most aggravating part of slicing, dicing, peeling, and paring is the messy mound of seeds, skins, rinds, and juice that gets left behind. When you try to scrape the trimmings into the trash, they slip over the boards' sides onto the floor or dribble all over the counter. This cutting board, however, sends the leftovers right where they belong—into the sink. As you work at the board, just push the unwanted extras through the hole.

Materials List

Maple, walnut, and cherry are recommended for this project.

(9)	7/8" x 1" x 23"	Maple strips
(2)	7/8" x 1" x 23"	Walnut strips
(2)	7/8" x 1" x 23"	Cherry strips
(2)	7/8" x 1/2" x 23"	Cherry strips

Suggested Tools

Router
3/8" roundover bit
3/8" drill
3/8" drill bit
Jigsaw
Pipe clamps
Compass
Try square
36" straightedge
Sander
Table saw

Hardware & Supplies

Waterproof wood glue
Food-grade bowl finish

Construction Procedure

1. The strips should be arranged so that their 1" dimensions represent the board's thickness. Using the illustration as a guide, and working from left to right, lay out the strips as follows: one 1/2"-wide cherry, six 7/8"-wide maple, six 7/8"-wide pieces of cherry, walnut, maple, walnut, cherry, and maple (in that order), one 1/2"-wide cherry, and a 7/8"-wide piece of maple.

2. Spread glue evenly on all the edges to be joined, and clamp the pieces together evenly and squarely. Let the glue dry overnight; sand the assembly smooth once the glue has dried.

3. Trim the board to 12-3/8" x 22-1/2" dimensions.

4. On each corner, measure and mark 2" in from both edges. Use these points to mark a 2" radius on each corner (see Layout Detail).

5. With the 1/2" cherry strip at the top, measure and mark 4-5/8" in from the left edge and 3-1/4" down from the top edge. At the point where those two lines intersect, use a compass set at a 2-1/16" radius to draw a 4-1/8"-diameter circle.

6. Drill a 3/8" hole near the inner edge of the circle, and use a jigsaw to cut the circle from the board. Sand the cut edge smooth.

7. Use the 3/8" roundover bit in the router to round every edge of the board and the circle.

8. Sand the board lightly, and finish the wood with a food-grade bowl finish.

LAYOUT DETAIL

4⅝"

3¼"

2"

4⅛"

2⅜"

22½"

OVER-THE-SINK CUTTING BOARD

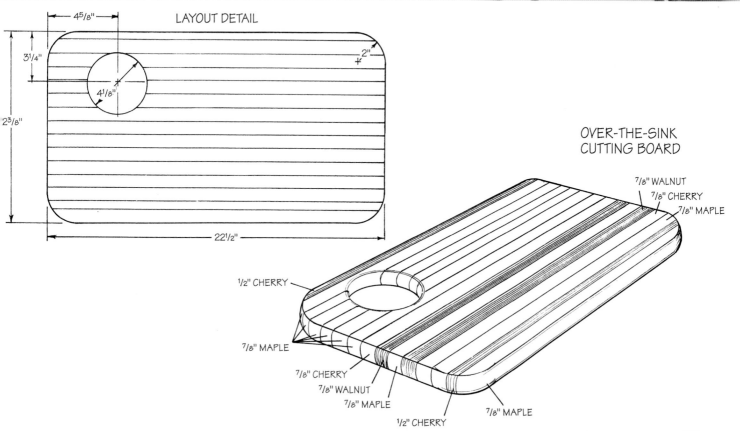

⅞" WALNUT
⅞" CHERRY
⅞" MAPLE

½" CHERRY

⅞" MAPLE

⅞" CHERRY
⅞" WALNUT
⅞" MAPLE

½" CHERRY

⅞" MAPLE

37

Vegetable Drying Rack

Why bother to dry your freshly washed vegetables by hand when you can use this drying rack instead? Spread your rinsed produce on the rack's dowels, and say goodbye to bruised lettuce and soggy kitchen towels. Designed to fit across a standard kitchen sink, the rack lets rinsed vegetables drain and dry naturally.

Materials List

Maple is recommended for this project.

(2)	3/4" x 2-1/2" x 15"	Rack sides
(2)	3/4" x 2-1/2" x 10"	Rack ends
(1)	3/4" x 2-1/2" x 38"	Legs
(21)	5/16" x 11-1/4"	Birch dowels

Suggested Tools

3/8" drill
5/16" drill bit
No. 8 pilot bit and countersink with stop collar
Router
3/8" roundover bit
Jigsaw
Compass
36" straightedge
Try square
No. 2 Phillips screwdriver

Hardware & Supplies

Waterproof wood glue
No. 8 x 1" flathead wood screws
16-gauge x 1-1/4" brads
3/8" dowel plugs
Spray lacquer

Construction Procedure

1. Measure down 1" from the edge of one 15" rack side, and strike a lengthwise line.

2. Measure 1-1/4" from the left end of the piece, and make a mark on the line. Measure 5/8" over from that point, and make a second mark. Continue until there are a total of twenty-one marks on the rack side.

3. With 1-1/4" brads placed in the corners, tack the two 2-1/2" x 15" rack sides together so that their edges are flush and the marks are on an outside face.

4. Use a 5/16" drill bit to bore holes through both pieces of wood at each of the twenty-one centers. Remove the brads, and then sand both pieces.

5. The rack frame will be assembled by butting the two drilled rack sides against the ends of the two 2-1/2" x 10" rack ends. First, trim the ends of the twenty-one dowels so that none are longer than 11-1/4". Then slip the dowels into one of the drilled pieces, and carefully fit the other piece over the opposite dowel ends, working from one end to the other.

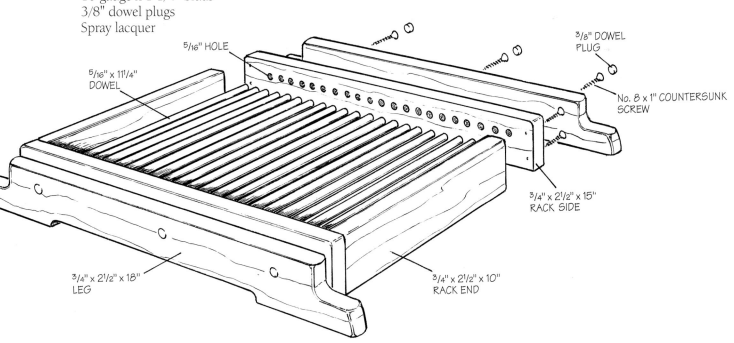

5/16" HOLE

3/8" DOWEL PLUG

5/16" x 11 1/4" DOWEL

No. 8 x 1" COUNTERSUNK SCREW

3/4" x 2 1/2" x 15" RACK SIDE

3/4" x 2 1/2" x 18" LEG

3/4" x 2 1/2" x 10" RACK END

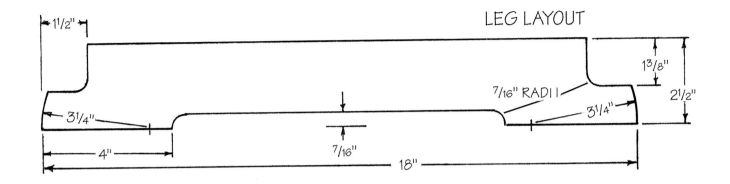

LEG LAYOUT

6. Position the two 10" rack ends, and then press the sides together. Fasten with No. 8 x 1" flathead screws, spaced 1-1/2" apart, inserted through the rack sides' faces and into the ends of the 10" rack pieces. Use the No. 8 pilot bit, setting the stop collar at 1-1/4". Plug the upper set of screw holes—the ones closest to the dowels—with 3/8" dowel plugs glued in place. Sand the plugs flush with the wood's surface.

7. Use a 3/8" roundover bit in the router to round all the edges of the assembled rack frame.

8. Cut the 2-1/2" x 38" strip into two 18" leg pieces. To mark the legs' outlines, refer to the Leg Layout illustration as you read the following instructions. First, measure 1-1/2" from each end on both pieces, and strike lines across their widths. Measure down 1-3/8" from each top edge, and mark a lengthwise line. Then, from each upper corner, mark a diagonal line to each (nearest) set of intersecting lines.

9. From the point at which each diagonal crosses its set of intersecting lines, measure 7/8" back up along the diagonal line, toward the board's upper corner, and mark a point on the diagonal. Using this point as a pivot for your compass, strike a 7/16" radius between the intersecting lines.

10. Next, strike a 3-1/4" radius at the legs' lower corners, using the lower edge of the board as a center line.

11. On the lower edge of each piece, measure 4" from each end, and make a mark. Then strike a 7/16" radius to intersect with each 4" mark by placing the compass point on the same edge, at a point 4-7/16" from the lower corner. Connect the ends of each pair of radii with a straight line drawn 7/16" from the lower edge.

12. Use a jigsaw to cut on the marked outlines.

13. With a 3/8" roundover bit in the router, round all the edges on both sides of each leg piece. Sand the pieces lightly.

14. Mount the legs to the dowel frame so that 1/2" of the frame protrudes above the upper edges of the legs. Use the No. 8 pilot bit to drill holes 5-1/4" apart and 1" from the upper edge of each leg, three in each side. Set the stop collar at 1-1/4". Fasten the legs with No. 8 x 1" flathead screws.

15. Plug the screw holes with 3/8" dowel plugs glued in place, and then sand the plugs flush with the legs' surfaces.

16. Finish the project with several coats of spray lacquer.

17. To use your vegetable drying rack, just flip it upside down so that the inner contours on each leg fit over the rim of your kitchen sink.

Adjustable Cookbook Stand

Tired of having to scrape 3-D fingerprints and last month's chocolate fudge off the recipes in your cookbooks? Build this useful cookbook stand instead. Its acrylic pegs are more than decorative; by placing them in the proper holes, you can keep any size book open—without using your hands.

Materials List

Walnut and cherry are recommended for this project.

(2)	3/4" x 5-3/8" x 19"	Cherry strips
(1)	3/4" x 1-3/8" x 19"	Walnut strip
(1)	3/4" x 3" x 19"	Walnut ledge
(1)	3/4" x 6" x 26"	Cherry legs
(1)	1/4" x 10"	Acrylic rods

Suggested Tools

3/8" drill
1/4" drill bit
No. 8 pilot bit and countersink with stop collar
Router
3/8" roundover bit
Pipe clamps
Jigsaw
Coping saw
Palm sander
Square
No. 2 Phillips screwdriver
Tack hammer
36" straightedge
Smooth file

Hardware & Supplies

Yellow wood glue
No. 8 x 1" flathead wood screws
3/8" dowel plugs
Spray lacquer

Construction Procedure

1. Spread glue evenly on the adjoining edges of the 1-3/8" walnut and 5-3/8" cherry strips. Clamp them squarely, and use a square to check for level. Allow the glue to dry overnight, and then sand both surfaces. Trim to 18-5/8" in length.

2. On both ends of the glued-up piece, measure 3/4" up from one long edge, and mark lines on both the front and back. Then use a 3/8" roundover bit to round the side and top edges of both faces, except for the 3/4" areas marked. Sand the edges well.

3. With the same router bit, round both ends and one edge on both faces of the 3" x 19" walnut ledge. Measure 1-5/8" and 2-3/8" from the ledge's square edge, and mark lines lengthwise. Next, measure 2", 3-1/2", and 5" from each end, and mark those points on both lines (see Ledge Detail).

4. Drill 1/4" holes, 1/4" deep at each of these twelve points. Sand both surfaces and the edges of the ledge.

5. Mount the ledge to the square 18-5/8" edge of the glued-up board so that it is centered between the board's ends. Use the No. 8 pilot bit to drill three holes, spaced 8-1/2" apart, through the ledge's bottom face and into the edge of the board. Set the stop collar at 1-1/4". Use No. 8 x 1" flathead screws to attach the ledge to the glued-up board.

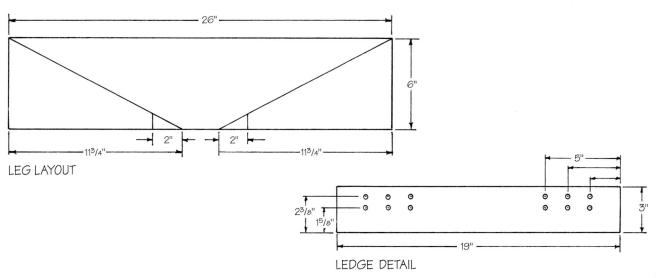

LEG LAYOUT

LEDGE DETAIL

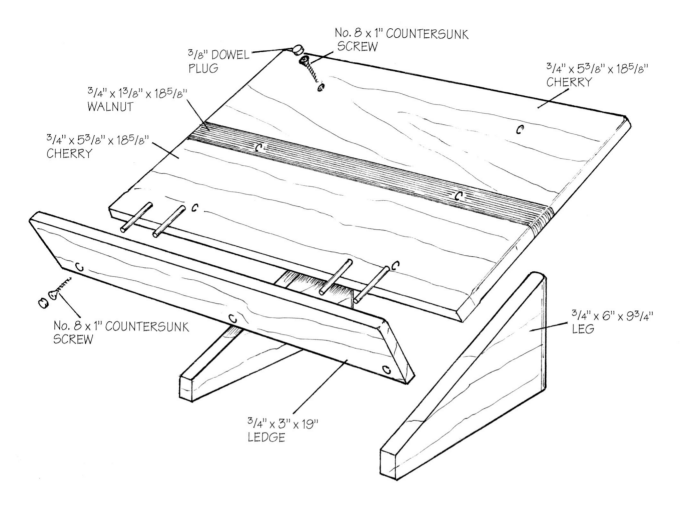

No. 8 x 1" COUNTERSUNK SCREW

3/8" DOWEL PLUG

3/4" x 1 3/8" x 18 5/8" WALNUT

3/4" x 5 3/8" x 18 5/8" CHERRY

3/4" x 5 3/8" x 18 5/8" CHERRY

No. 8 x 1" COUNTERSUNK SCREW

3/4" x 3" x 19" LEDGE

3/4" x 6" x 9 3/4" LEG

6. From each end of the 26" cherry piece, measure in 11-3/4" along one edge, and mark (see Leg Layout). Strike a diagonal from each upper corner to the mark closest to it. Then, along the piece's bottom edge, measure 2" outward from each marked point, and use a square to strike a line to meet the diagonal.

7. Cut the diagonals with a jigsaw, and then trim the 2" corners from each of the leg pieces.

8. With a 3/8" roundover bit in the router, round both faces of the 6" edge on each leg. Sand all sides and edges.

9. Measure 3-3/4" from each end of the 18-5/8" board, and strike a light line across its width on the face and back at those points. Measure 1/2" from the rounded top edge on the back, and mark a line.

10. Use these marks to align the legs prior to drilling the screw holes. The 6" edge of each leg should be set at the 1/2" marks on the back. Use a No. 8 pilot bit to drill holes, spaced 4-1/2" apart, through the face of the board and into the edges of the legs beneath. Set the stop collar at 1-1/4". Use No. 8 x 1" screws to attach the legs.

11. Plug all screw holes with 3/8" dowel plugs glued in place. Sand the plugs flush with the wood's surface.

12. Sand the project lightly, and finish the wood with several coats of spray lacquer.

13. Use a coping saw to cut the acrylic rod to four 2-1/4" lengths. Round the ends of each cut piece with the smooth-cut file. Place the rods in the appropriate sockets for the size book being held.

Folding Cookbook Stand

Attach this stand to a wall next to the area where you do most of your measuring and mixing. Then, whenever you need to hold open your cookbook, pull the stand away from the wall, and its prop board will drop down to brace the stand at a convenient angle. When you're through, just fold the prop back, and the stand will rest flat against the wall again.

Materials List

White or red oak is recommended for this project.

(4)	3/4" x 3-5/16" x 19"	Top
(1)	3/4" x 7-1/2" x 15"	Prop board
(1)	3/4" x 1-1/8" x 18-3/4"	Bottom rail
(1)	3/4" x 3-1/16" x 6"	Pivot arms
(1)	3/4" x 3-1/16" x 10"	Mounting blocks
(1)	5/8" x 36"	Birch dowel

Suggested Tools

Table saw
3/8" drill
5/64" and 3/16" drill bits
5/8" spade bit
No. 8 pilot bit and countersink with stop collar
Router
3/8" roundover bit
1/2" straight bit
Jigsaw
Compass
36" straightedge
No. 2 Phillips screwdriver
3/16" straight blade screwdriver
Pipe clamps
Try square
Palm sander

Hardware & Supplies

Yellow wood glue
1-1/4"-diameter wooden balls (2)
1-1/4" x 14" piano hinge
No. 5 x 3/4" flathead brass screws
4-gauge x 2-3/16" screw eyes (2)
No. 8 x 1" flathead wood screws
No. 8 x 1-1/2" flathead wood screws
Spray lacquer

Construction Procedure

1. To make the stand's top piece, spread glue evenly on adjoining edges of the four 3-5/16" x 19" boards. Clamp the pieces together squarely and evenly, and allow the glue to dry overnight. Sand both surfaces.

2. With a table saw, trim the glued-up top to 12-13/16" x 18-3/4" dimensions.

3. On both faces of the top piece, measure up 1" from an 18-3/4" edge, and strike lines lengthwise. Using a 3/8" roundover bit in the router, round three edges on both faces of the top, down to the 1" marks. Sand the top's edges.

4. On the 1-1/8" x 18-3/4" bottom rail, round both sides of one edge. Clamp the rail to the top (at its non-routed edge) so that the rail's lower face is flush with the top's bottom edge. Then drill four holes, spaced 5-1/4" apart, through the top's back and into the bottom rail's edge. Use the No. 8 pilot bit, setting the stop collar at 1". Fasten the rail with No. 8 x 1" flathead screws.

5. On the top piece's upper edge, measure and mark 5" in from each end. At each mark, drill a 3/16" hole to a depth of 1". Next, use the tip of a straight-bladed screwdriver to open the eyes of the two screw eyes enough to accommodate the 5/8" dowel. Then fasten the screw eyes to the top piece's edge so that their eye-holes are aligned.

6. On the top's back face, measure up 4-3/4" from the bottom edge, and strike a line the length of the board. Center the piano hinge at this line so that its screw holes are on the line (see Side View). The hinge should close toward the top of the top piece, and its pin should face toward the bottom. Use a 5/64" drill bit to make the mounting holes, and mount the hinge with No. 5 x 3/4" flathead screws.

7. On the 3-1/6" x 10" piece, use a straight bit in the router to dado a 3/4"-wide, 3/8"-deep slot down the center of one face. Round both long edges of this face, using a 3/8" roundover bit in the router. Cut the piece into two 4" lengths to make the two mounting blocks.

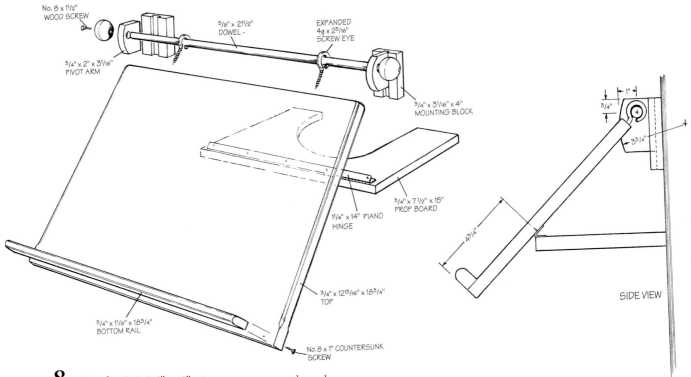

No. 8 x 1 1/2"
WOOD SCREW

5/8" x 21 1/2"
DOWEL

EXPANDED
4g x 2 3/16"
SCREW EYE

3/4" x 2" x 3 1/16"
PIVOT ARM

3/4" x 3 1/16" x 4"
MOUNTING BLOCK

1 1/4" x 14" PIANO
HINGE

3/4" x 7 1/2" x 15"
PROP BOARD

3/4" x 12 13/16" x 18 3/4"
TOP

3/4" x 1 1/8" x 18 3/4"
BOTTOM RAIL

No. 8 x 1" COUNTERSUNK
SCREW

1"

3/4"

3 3/4"

4 3/4"

SIDE VIEW

8. On the 3-1/16" x 6" piece, measure and mark two lines, 2" in from each end. Then strike a center line down the length of the board.

9. From the center line, strike a 3-3/4" radius at each end of the piece.

10. From each 2" line, measure 1" toward the radius and mark a line across the piece. On each end of the piece, measure down 3/4" from one edge, and mark along the piece. Where each set of marks intersects, use a 5/8" spade bit to drill a hole through the piece (see Side View).

11. Use a jigsaw to cut the radius line at each end. Cut the piece at the 2" lines to create two 2" x 3-1/16" pivot arms. Sand the cut edges and the holes smooth.

12. Position the two pivot arms in the dadoes of the two mounting blocks so that the top edges are flush. Use a No. 8 pilot bit to drill through the back of the mounting blocks and into the pivot arms. Set the stop collar at 1". Fasten the supports with No. 8 x 1" flat-head wood screws.

13. Cut the dowel to 21-1/2" in length, and drill a 1/2"-deep hole in the center of each end, using the No. 8 pilot bit. Slide the dowel through the screw eyes; then slip the pivot arms over each end of the dowel.

14. Set the stop collar at 1-1/2", and drill a hole through the center of each 1-1/4" wooden ball. Fasten the balls to the ends of the dowel with No. 8 x 1-1/2" flathead wood screws.

15. Find the center of the 7-1/2" x 15" prop board piece, and strike a line across the board's width, using a square. From one long edge, measure down 1-1/4", and mark on the line. Use this point as a center to strike a 3-3/4"-radius half-circle across the line. Use the square again to strike lines between the ends of the half-circle and the edge of the board (see the Folding Cooking Stand illustration for location of this marked shape).

16. With a jigsaw, cut out the marked section.

17. Use the 3/8" roundover bit in the router to round both edges of the 7-1/2" ends and the inside edge of the cut radius. Sand the board and the cut edges.

18. Mount the finished prop board to the hinge with No. 5 x 3/4" flathead screws. The cut opening should face away from the stand's top piece.

19. Sand the project lightly, and finish with several coats of spray lacquer.

Butcher Block Table

This project offers more than a traditional, butcher-block cutting surface. Its lower shelf will store your bowls, its handles will air your kitchen towels, and its cutting block is removable. Whether you chop and dice, mix and knead, or pack the children's lunches on it, this table is likely to become a treasured part of your kitchen.

Materials List

Maple and white oak are recommended for this project.

(23)	3/4" x 1-7/8" x 28"	Maple top strips
(2)	3/4" x 1-7/8" x 27-7/16"	Maple upper side supports
(2)	3/4" x 1-7/8" x 15-9/16"	Maple upper end supports
(4)	3/4" x 2" x 35-1/2"	Oak legs
(4)	3/4" x 2-3/4" x 35-1/2"	Oak legs
(2)	3/4" x 2-1/2" x 27-7/16"	Oak lower side supports
(2)	3/4" x 2-1/2" x 15-9/16"	Oak lower end supports
(12)	3/4" x 1-3/8" x 17"	Oak shelf slats

Suggested Tools

Table saw
3/8" drill
No. 8 pilot bit and countersink with stop collar
Router
1/4" roundover bit
Pipe clamps
36" straightedge
Compass
Jigsaw
Belt sander
Square
No. 2 Phillips screwdriver

Hardware & Supplies

Waterproof wood glue
No. 8 x 1" flathead wood screws
3/4" x 1-3/8" corner braces
3/8" dowel plugs
3/8" roundtop plugs
Spray lacquer
Food-grade bowl finish

Construction Procedure

1. The surface of the table is made from 3/4" x 1-7/8" maple strips glued together. Apply glue evenly to the 1-7/8" sides of the strips to be joined, and clamp the assembly together. Check with a framing square to assure that the surface is level and that the corners are square. (You'll find it easier to keep the strips aligned if you glue them together in four- or five-piece sections.) Once the assembly is ready, trim it to the final dimensions of 17-1/16" x 27-7/16".

2. Fasten the 2" x 35-1/2" leg pieces to the 2-3/4" x 35-1/2" leg pieces so that both faces measure 2-3/4" across. Use a No. 8 pilot bit and countersink (with the stop collar set at 1-1/4") to drill holes through the wider board's face and into the edge of the narrower board. Space the holes 10" apart on each leg, and use No. 8 x 1" flathead wood screws to fasten the leg pieces together.

3. With a 1/4" roundover bit, rout all the outside edges of each completed leg. Sand all sides and corners smooth.

4. To locate the placement of the lower supports, measure and mark 14" up from the inside bottom end of each leg.

5. Fasten the 27-7/16" lower side supports to the inside of each set of legs, using No. 8 x 1" flathead wood screws inserted through the inside faces of the supports. Position the top edge of each board flush with the 14" mark. Set the stop collar on the No. 8 pilot bit and countersink to 1-1/4".

6. Fasten the 15-9/16" lower end supports to the legs, between the pieces just placed. Make sure that their edges are flush with those of the lower side supports. Use No. 8 x 1" screws, and mount as before.

7. On the top edge of this frame, mount the twelve 1-3/8" x 17" oak shelf slats. Place the end slats first, snug against the leg assemblies. Using a No. 8 pilot bit, with the stop collar set at 1", drill through the slats and into the supports' edges. Fasten the slats with No. 8 x 1" flathead screws. Secure the remaining ten slats, using a scrap of 1"-thick wood as a spacer to position them.

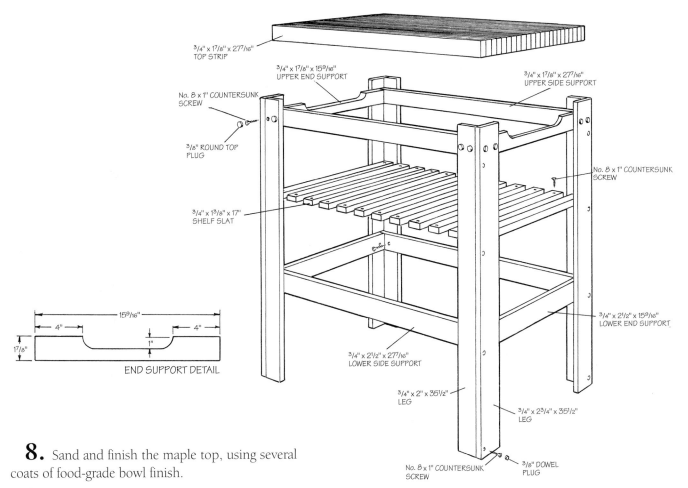

³/4" x 1⁷/8" x 27⁷/16"
TOP STRIP

³/4" x 1⁷/8" x 15⁹/16"
UPPER END SUPPORT

No. 8 x 1" COUNTERSUNK
SCREW

³/8" ROUND TOP
PLUG

³/4" x 1⁷/8" x 27⁷/16"
UPPER SIDE SUPPORT

No. 8 x 1" COUNTERSUNK
SCREW

³/4" x 1³/8" x 17"
SHELF SLAT

15⁹/16"

4"   4"

1⁷/8"   1"

END SUPPORT DETAIL

³/4" x 2¹/2" x 15⁹/16"
LOWER END SUPPORT

³/4" x 2¹/2" x 27⁷/16"
LOWER SIDE SUPPORT

³/4" x 2" x 35¹/2"
LEG

³/4" x 2³/4" x 35¹/2"
LEG

No. 8 x 1" COUNTERSUNK
SCREW

³/8" DOWEL
PLUG

8. Sand and finish the maple top, using several coats of food-grade bowl finish.

9. On the top edge of each of the two 1-7/8" x 15-9/16" upper end support pieces, measure and mark 4" and 5" in from each end. Using the 5" marks as centers, strike a 1" radius that meets with each 4" mark. Then strike a straight line to join the two radius ends on each piece (see End Support Detail).

10. With a jigsaw, cut the marked line on each upper end support. Then use a 1/4" roundover bit to round the edges of the cut. Sand the pieces smooth. Use the sander to smooth the 27-7/16" upper side supports as well.

11. Align the upper side supports with their top edges 2-1/8" below the top of each leg, and fasten them to the inside of the legs. Use a No. 8 pilot bit to drill holes from the outside, spaced 1-1/4" apart. Set the stop collar to 1-1/4", and use No. 8 x 1" flathead screws.

12. Attach the 15-9/16" upper end supports to the legs in the same manner. The relief cuts should face upward.

13. If you wish the table surface to be permanently mounted, position it on the upper supports, and fasten it to them with four 3/4" x 1-3/8" corner braces, using the hardware provided. (The maple top's surface will rest 1/4" below the top edges of each leg.) If you'd prefer a removable table surface, do not attach the top; simply drop it in place onto the supports.

14. Plug all the screw holes with 3/8" dowel plugs glued in place. The sixteen plugs over the upper supports' screws should be a roundtop style. Sand all the others flat.

15. If the oil-finished top is permanently affixed, tape newspaper over it before finishing the remainder of the wood frame with several coats of spray lacquer. If the top isn't fastened in place with corner braces, just remove it before applying the lacquer.

Utensil Rack

Keeping your corkscrews, vegetable peelers, fondue forks, and mixing spoons stuffed into crowded drawers isn't good for them—or for you. The drawers jam, tools bend or break, and fingers get stabbed as they probe the depths. Instead, try storing your utensils where you can see and reach them easily; this handy rack can be hung on a wall or placed on any counter.

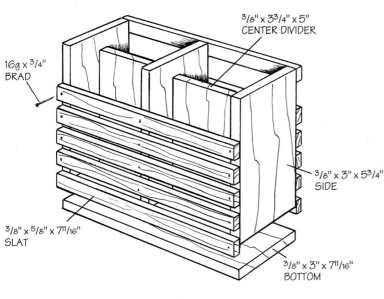

3/8" x 3-3/4" x 5"
CENTER DIVIDER

16g x 3/4"
BRAD

3/8" x 3" x 5-3/4"
SIDE

3/8" x 5/8" x 7-11/16"
SLAT

3/8" x 3" x 7-11/16"
BOTTOM

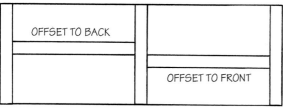

OFFSET TO BACK

OFFSET TO FRONT

DIVIDER PLACEMENT

Materials List

Cypress is recommended for this project.

(3)	3/8" x 3" x 5-3/4"	Sides and center board
(2)	3/8" x 3-3/4" x 5"	Center dividers
(11)	3/8" x 5/8" x 7-11/16"	Slats
(1)	3/8" x 3" x 7-11/16"	Bottom

Suggested Tools

Tack hammer
Nail set
12" straightedge

Hardware & Supplies

Yellow wood glue
16-gauge x 3/4" brads
Spray lacquer

Construction Procedure

1. Sand the surfaces of all the wooden pieces.

2. On both sides of one 3" x 5-3/4" piece and on one side of the other two, strike a line lengthwise down the center. The piece with two center lines will be the center board.

3. Use a couple of brads to nail one long edge of a 3-3/4" x 5" center divider to the center board. Offset the center divider so that its front face is even with the marked line on the board, and make sure that the divider's bottom edge is flush with the board's bottom end. Then nail the second 3-3/4" x 5" center divider to the board's opposite side; this time, offset the divider so that its back face is even with the line (see Divider Placement).

4. Position the face of a 3" x 5-3/4" side piece on the end of one center divider so that the divider's edge is centered on top of the marked line on the side piece. Check to see that the bottom ends of both pieces are flush.

5. Nail the last side piece to the other divider in the same manner.

6. Nail the 3" x 7-11/16" bottom to the assembly's flush end.

7. Starting from the bottom, glue and nail five slats into place on each side of the assembly; the bottom slat should be flush with the bottom of the base. Leave 1/4" between each slat, and center one brad per joint.

8. Fasten the last slat flush with the top edge on one side of the assembly.

9. Set all the outside brads with the nail set. Sand the wood lightly.

10. Finish the project with several coats of spray lacquer.

Spoon Rack

Counter tops are especially susceptible to that dread disease, "creeping clutter." When your kitchen drawers are full and your utensils start to invade horizontal surfaces, you can clear some space by attaching this spoon rack to a convenient wall. Hang it with its decorative edge facing either up or down.

Materials List

Red or yellow cypress is recommended for this project.

(1)   3/4" x 4-1/2" x 18"   Mounting board
(1)   1/2" x 1" x 16-1/2"   Rack

Suggested Tools

Jigsaw
3/8" drill
Router
Compass
36" straightedge
No. 8 pilot bit and counterbore with stop collar
No. 2 Phillips screwdriver
1/2" drill bit
1/4" roundover bit

Hardware & Supplies

Yellow wood glue
No. 8 x 1" flathead wood screws
Spray lacquer
18" x 22" piece of cardboard

Construction Procedure

1. On the 16-1/2" rack piece, mark a center line lengthwise down the face.

2. Measure in 2" from one end, and mark on the line. At a point 2-1/2" from this mark, make another mark. Continue to measure and mark at 2-1/2" intervals until there are a total of six marks along the line.

3. Drill 1/2" holes at the six marked centers.

4. To round the ends of the rack, measure in 1" from each end, and make a mark on one edge of the rack's face. Using these marks, strike a 1" radius at each end. Then cut the marked curves with a jigsaw.

5. On the 18" mounting board, mark the center at 9". Next, set your compass to a 21-1/2" radius. Placing the compass at the center point of one 18" edge of the cardboard piece, draw a 21-1/2" radius. Cut the cardboard along the marked radius line, and flip it upside down. Then align the center of the cut arc's edge with the center of the mounting board's bottom edge, and transfer the arc to the bottom of the board's face (see Mounting Board Detail).

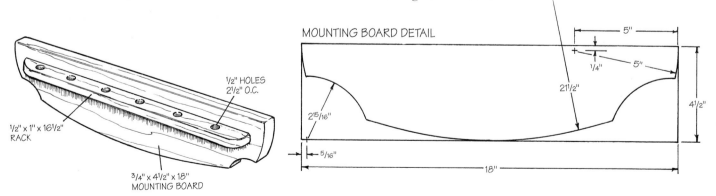

1/2" HOLES 2½" O.C.

1/2" x 1" x 16½" RACK

3/4" x 4½" x 18" MOUNTING BOARD

MOUNTING BOARD DETAIL

5"

1/4"

5"

21½"

4½"

2¹⁵/₁₆"

5/16"

18"

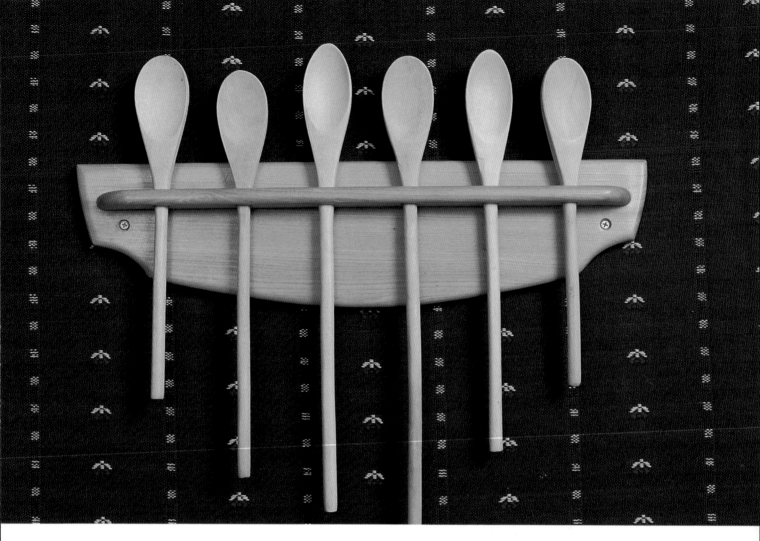

6. Measure in 5/16" from each bottom corner of the mounting board, and strike a 2-15/16" radius across each lower quadrant (see Mounting Board Detail).

7. Measure in 5" from each upper corner, and make a mark. Then measure down 1/4" from each of these marks, and strike a 5" radius between the upper edge of the wood and each 2-15/16" radius just drawn.

8. With a jigsaw, cut all the radii as marked, and sand the wood smooth.

9. Using a 1/4" roundover bit in the router, round both sides of the racks's three exposed edges. The fourth edge should be left square; it will be fastened against the back and will not be exposed. Then round all edges of the mounting board's face side. Sand the wood lightly.

10. Measure 7/8" down from the top (flat) edge of the mounting board, and mark a line across its back

surface. Measure in 1-3/4" from each end, and mark at the line.

11. Align the rack with the mounting board's face. With a No. 8 pilot hole and counterbore, drill two holes at the two marked points, through the board and into the rack. Set the stop collar at a 1-1/8" depth.

12. Spread glue along the back edge of the rack, and fasten it to the mounting board with No. 8 x 1" flathead wood screws.

13. From the face side of the mounting board, drill countersunk No. 8-screw mounting holes, 1" below the holes for the shelf screws and centered 16" apart.

14. Sand lightly and finish with three or more coats of spray lacquer.

Upright Knife Block

Like the Adjustable Knife Block, this one will protect your knives' blades and provide a convenient storage spot, but it uses less space and is a bit easier to construct. You can tailor the slots to suit your knives by adjusting the grooves' depths as you cut them. And if you own a sharpening steel, you can rout a special slot for it.

Materials List

White pine is recommended for this project.

(6) 3/4" x 5" x 12-1/2"   Sheath blocks
(4) 3/4" x 7/8" x 4-1/2"   Retaining blocks

Suggested Tools

Table saw
Handsaw
3/8" drill
Try square
Pipe clamps
12" straightedge
No. 6 pilot bit and countersink with stop collar
No. 2 Phillips screwdriver

Hardware & Supplies

Yellow wood glue
No. 6 x 3/4" brass flathead wood screws
Spray lacquer

Construction Procedure

1. Spread glue evenly over the faces of the six 5" x 12-1/2" boards. Clamp them together, checking the alignment of their ends and sides with your square.

2. Scrape any excess glue off the sheath block, and then trim the ends square on the table saw.

3. On both sides of the sheath block's 4-1/2" sides, mark and cut full-length slots every 3/4". On one side, starting from the left, the first two cuts should be 1-3/4" deep, the next two 1-1/2" deep, and the final one 1-1/4" deep. On the opposite side, the cut furthest to the left should be 1-1/4" deep and the remaining four should be 1" in depth (see Kerf Detail).

4. Lay the sheath block on a surface so that the shallowest slots are to the left and the 5" face is showing. From the top left corner, measure over 2" and down 2-3/4". Mark the edges at these points, and then strike a line between them.

5. Use a square to transfer this line around the sheath block's four surfaces.

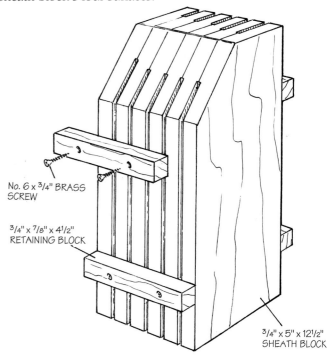

No. 6 x 3/4" BRASS SCREW

3/4" x 7/8" x 4-1/2" RETAINING BLOCK

3/4" x 5" x 12½" SHEATH BLOCK

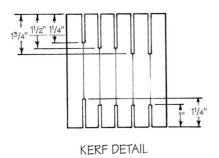

1¾" 1½" 1¼"

1" 1¼"

KERF DETAIL

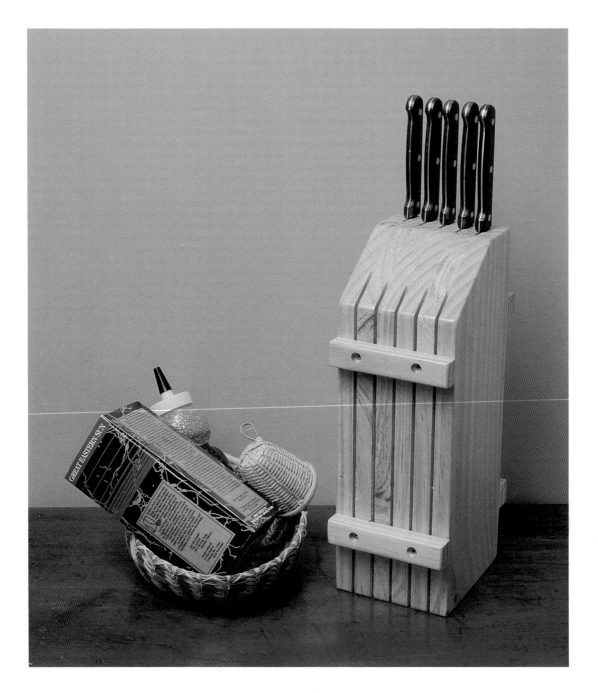

6. With a handsaw, cut the corner from the block, using the line as a guide. Check the path of cut for accuracy as you progress.

7. Measuring from the bottom edge of the angled 4-1/2" side, strike two lines across the slotted face, one at 2" and another at 8-3/8". Repeat this process on the opposite 4-1/2" side, but this time mark the second line at 9-1/8".

8. Center the 4-1/2" retaining blocks over the lines, with their 3/4" faces outward, and mark the screw holes 1-1/8" apart. Use the No. 6 pilot bit to drill through each retaining block and into the sheath block. Set the stop collar at 1". Attach the retaining blocks with No. 6 x 3/4" brass flat-head wood screws.

9. Sand the project, rounding all edges slightly.

10. Finish the knife block with several coats of spray lacquer.

Adjustable Knife Block

Because the knife slots in this block extend through both its ends, it can be set up in two different positions. If you have plenty of counter space, you can rest the block horizontally; the long edges of the leg assembly will raise the knives at a slight angle. In cramped quarters, you can save space by reversing the block and placing it upright (as we have in the photograph) so that the handles of your knives are almost vertical.

Materials List

White or red oak is recommended for this project.

(2)	1" x 9-1/4" x 12-1/2"	Blocks
(1)	3/4" x 4-1/4" x 12-1/2"	Legs
(1)	3/4" x 3" x 12"	Support

Hint: *If you're sure your block will always be in a vertical position, you can make it more stable by adding 1/2" to the length of the legs and support; the leg assembly's ends will then rest flush with the block's bottom.*

Suggested Tools

Circular saw
3/8" drill
Try square
36" straightedge
No. 2 Phillips screwdriver
No. 8 pilot bit and countersink with stop collar
C-clamps

Hardware & Supplies

Yellow wood glue
No. 8 x 1" flathead wood screws
No. 8 x 1-1/4" flathead wood screws
3/8" dowel plugs
Spray lacquer

Construction Procedure

1. Clamp the two blocks together, face to face.

2. Locate the knife-blade grooves by measuring and marking eight lines, centered 1" apart, across one end of the clamped assembly.

3. Separate the blocks. Use a square to transfer the eight marked lines to one face of each section.

4. Set the circular saw blade at a 13/16" depth, and cut a full-length slot in both blocks at the first and second marks.

5. For the third cut, set the blade at a depth of 3/4", and slot each block as before.

6. Make the fourth and fifth cuts with the blade set at a 5/8" depth.

7. Set the blade depth at 1/2" to make the final three cuts.

8. Slide a piece of folded sandpaper down each slot to remove slivers and burrs.

9. Re-clamp the blocks together with the matching slots facing each other. Keep the assembly as aligned as possible.

10. Next, select one face of the block to serve as its back. Then, using the No. 8 pilot bit and a stop collar set at 1-1/2", drill four holes along each side of that face. Space these at equal distances and 1/2" in from the edges. Drill four more holes down the center of the block.

11. Fasten the two blocks together with No. 8 x 1-1/4" flathead wood screws. Wax the screw threads if necessary to prevent binding.

12. Cover the eight screw holes by gluing 3/8" dowel plugs in them. Sand the plugs flat.

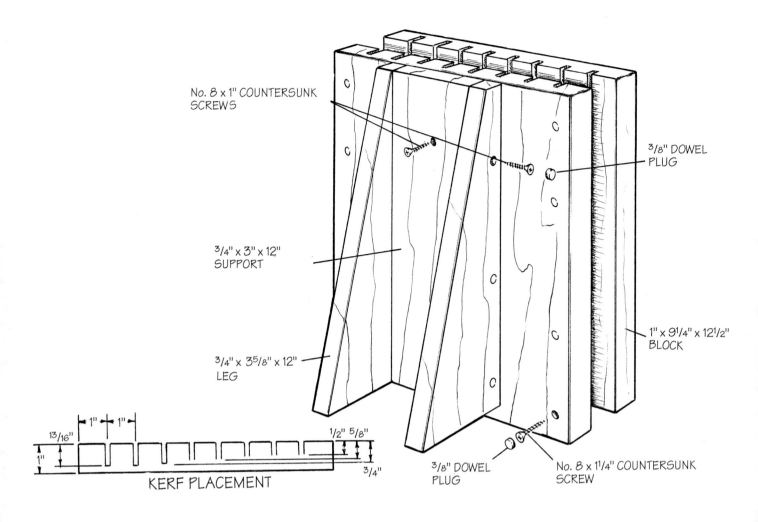

No. 8 x 1" COUNTERSUNK SCREWS

3/4" x 3" x 12" SUPPORT

3/4" x 3⁵/₈" x 12" LEG

3/8" DOWEL PLUG

1" x 9¹/₄" x 12¹/₂" BLOCK

3/8" DOWEL PLUG

No. 8 x 1¹/₄" COUNTERSUNK SCREW

13/16"

1"

1" 1"

1/2" 5/8"

3/4"

KERF PLACEMENT

13. Mark a diagonal line across the 3/4" x 4-1/4" x 12-1/2" piece so that each end of the line is 5/8" from one long edge. Cut the board along this line.

14. Cut 1/2" off the narrow end of each board, and sand the two leg pieces lightly.

15. Place the two leg pieces against the long edges of the 3" x 12" support.

16. Mark three points on each outer leg face for screw holes, centering them about 4-1/2" apart.

17. Using the No. 8 pilot bit, drill three holes through each leg face and into the support. Set the stop collar at 1-1/4".

18. Fasten the legs to the support with No. 8 x 1" flathead wood screws.

19. Cover the screw holes with 3/8" dowel plugs glued in place. Sand the plugs flat.

20. Draw two parallel lines down the back face of the block assembly, each 2-3/8" from an edge.

21. Place the leg assembly between the lines so that its narrow end is flush with the block's top edge.

22. Using the No. 8 pilot bit (and a stop collar set at 1-1/4"), drill two holes 8" apart along the center of the support.

23. Attach the leg assembly to the block with No. 8 x 1" flathead wood screws.

24. Round off all edges with sandpaper, and sand the entire project lightly.

25. Finish with several coats of spray lacquer.

A Hanger for Pots and Pans

When kitchen storage space is at a premium, and you can't possibly squeeze in one more cupboard or shelf, don't worry. Stare into space instead—the space just below your kitchen ceiling! That's where you'll be hanging this elegant rack for pots and pans. Don't let its name imply that this project can only be used in one way; its hooks will hold anything from your favorite baskets to small bundles of dried herbs.

Materials List

Walnut and cypress are recommended for this project.

(2)	5/16" x 3/4" x 36"	Walnut insets
(2)	5/16" x 3/4" x 26"	Walnut insets
(2)	3/4" x 2-1/2" x 36"	Cypress side supports
(4)	3/4" x 2-1/2" x 26"	Cypress end supports and center supports

Suggested Tools

3/8" drill
No. 8 pilot bit and countersink with stop collar
1/16" and 1/4" drill bits
Router
3/8" roundover bit
1/2" straight bit
No. 2 Phillips screwdriver
Coping saw
Tack hammer
36" straightedge

Hardware & Supplies

Yellow wood glue
No. 8 x 1" flathead wood screws
18-gauge x 5/8" brads
000-gauge x 2-1/16" screw eyes (4)
1" brass cup hooks (30)
3/8" dowel plugs
Spray polyurethane

Construction Procedure

1. Use a straight bit in the router to cut a dado 5/16" deep and 3/4" wide down the center of two 2-1/2" x 26" cypress pieces. These two pieces will be the end supports. Rout a dado of the same dimensions down the center of the 2-1/2" x 36" cypress side supports.

2. Glue the walnut insets into the dado channels. (You may secure them with 5/8" brads if their fit is loose, but before doing so, read Step 8 regarding placement of the cup hooks.)

3. Sand the faces and edges on all four pieces.

4. Fasten the two side supports to the ends of the two 26" end supports with a pair of countersunk No. 8 x 1" flathead screws at each corner, spaced 1-5/8" apart. Use a No. 8 pilot bit to bore the holes, and set the stop collar at 1-1/4".

5. On each side support, measure 12" from each end, and mark the inside faces. These will be the center points for positioning the two 26" cypress center supports. Mount the center supports using the same method as in Step 4.

6. Plug all the screw holes with 3/8" dowel plugs glued in place. Sand the plugs flat with the wood's surface.

7. Using a 3/8" roundover bit in the router, round all edges of the assembled hanger, both inside and out. Take care to keep the router level while you work; it may help to make up a 2-1/2" x 11" box to use as a support at the inside portion of the hanger frame. Sand all surfaces when completed.

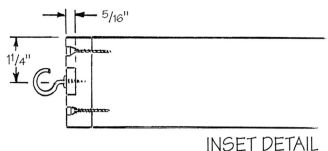

5/16"

1 1/4"

INSET DETAIL

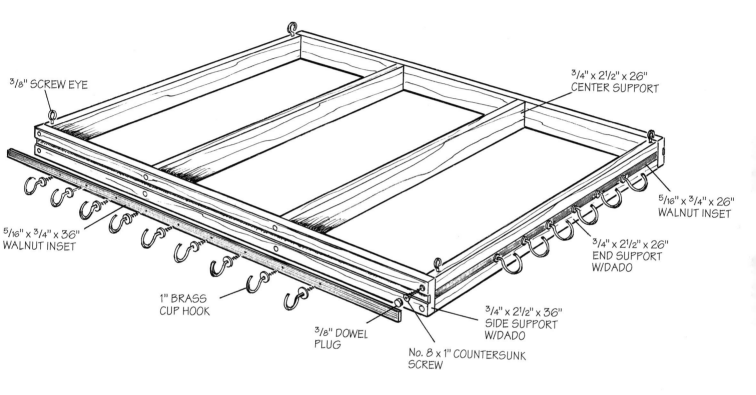

3/8" SCREW EYE

3/4" x 2¹/2" x 26"
CENTER SUPPORT

5/16" x 3/4" x 26"
WALNUT INSET

5/16" x 3/4" x 36"
WALNUT INSET

3/4" x 2¹/2" x 26"
END SUPPORT
W/DADO

1" BRASS
CUP HOOK

3/8" DOWEL
PLUG

3/4" x 2¹/2" x 36"
SIDE SUPPORT
W/DADO

No. 8 x 1" COUNTERSUNK
SCREW

8. On all four sides of the assembled frame, measure 1-1/4" down from each upper edge, and strike a light line the length of each walnut inset (see Inset Detail). Measure 6" from each frame corner (in both directions), and mark at the 1-1/4" center line. Mark centers for the side hooks every 3" between these 6" marks. Mark centers for the end hooks every 3-1/8".

9. Use a 1/16" drill bit to bore the thirty hook holes at the points marked. Be careful not to penetrate the frame while drilling.

10. On the top edge of both end supports, mark 1-3/4" in from each corner. Drill 1/4" holes at these points, to a depth of 1-1/2".

11. Finish the frame with several coats of spray polyurethane.

12. Fasten the cup hooks and screw eyes in place.

One-Step Stool

This unpretentious stool is one of our favorite projects. Though it won't fold up or miraculously turn into a baby's high chair, it does its job, looks good, and unlike more elaborate stools, doesn't hog space. What's more, when you're not using it to reach that awkward top shelf, this project is attractive enough to place right on the counter. You can even use it as a plant stand or book shelf!

Materials List

White or red oak is recommended for this project.

(2)	3/4" x 10" x 10"	Side supports
(1)	3/4" x 10" x 16"	Top
(1)	3/4" x 5-3/4" x 16-1/2"	Center support

Suggested Tools

Table saw
Jigsaw
3/8" drill
Half-round bastard file
36" straightedge
Compass
No. 2 Phillips screwdriver
No. 8 pilot bit and counterbore with stop collar
5/16" drill bit

Hardware & Supplies

Yellow wood glue
No. 8 x 1" flathead wood screws
3/8" dowel plugs
Spray polyurethane

Construction Procedure

1. Use the table saw to bevel the top and bottom edges of both 10" x 10" side supports at 25°, creating parallel bevels.

2. Bevel all edges of the 10" x 16" top at 25° so that the bottom face maintains its 10" x 16" dimensions.

3. On the 5-3/4" x 16-1/2" center support, measure and mark 1" in from the top corners. Then measure and mark 1/4" in from the bottom corners. Strike a line between the two marks at each end (see Center Support).

4. Use a jigsaw to cut along both lines, making a trapezoid shape with a 14-1/2" upper edge and a 16" lower edge.

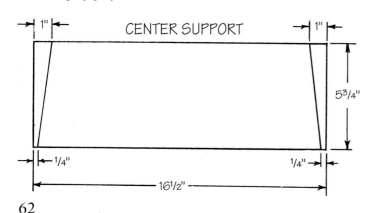

CENTER SUPPORT

1"   1"
5³/4"
1/4"   1/4"
16¹/2"

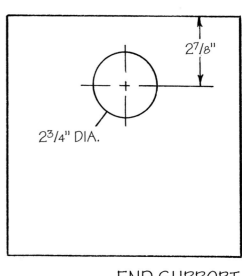

2⁷/8"
2³/4" DIA.

END SUPPORT

62

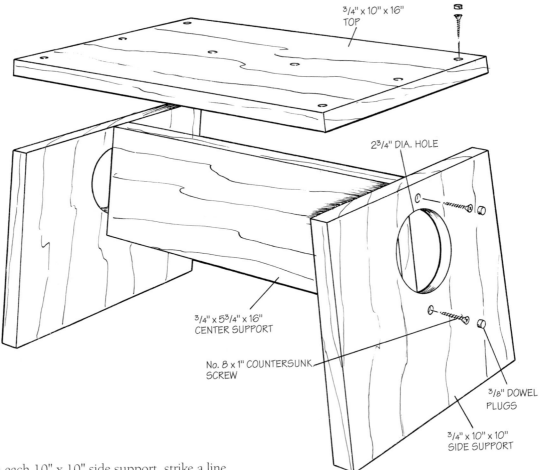

3/4" x 10" x 16"
TOP

2³/4" DIA. HOLE

3/4" x 5³/4" x 16"
CENTER SUPPORT

No. 8 x 1" COUNTERSUNK
SCREW

3/8" DOWEL
PLUGS

3/4" x 10" x 10"
SIDE SUPPORT

5. On each 10" x 10" side support, strike a line down the center. Then measure 2-7/8" down from each top edge, and make a mark on the center line. (Be sure to take all your measurements on the outer face of each board so that the beveled edges are consistent.) With the pivot of your compass at this point, make a 2-3/4"-diameter circle on the face of each piece (see End Support).

6. Drill a 5/16" hole through the wood near the inside edge of each circle. Then cut out each disk with a jigsaw, and smooth the edges of the holes with the half-round bastard file.

7. Sand the faces of each piece and the inside edges of the circular holes.

8. Place the top on the upper edges of the side supports so that its ends are flush with the supports' faces. Use the No. 8 pilot bit and counterbore to center three holes along each short end of the top's face, 4-1/4" apart; set the stop collar at 1-1/4" to leave room for the dowel plugs.

9. Spread glue on the mating surfaces of the side supports and top, and use No. 8 x 1" flathead wood screws to fasten them together.

10. Position the center support between the side supports, centering it beneath the top. With the No. 8 pilot bit and counterbore, center two holes 6" apart, through the face of the top. Make two more holes through each side support, 3/4" above and below the 2-3/4" openings cut earlier. Keep the stop collar set at 1-1/4" for these holes as well.

11. Apply glue to the edges of the center support, and fasten it to the top and side supports with No. 8 x 1" flathead wood screws. Plug all the recessed screw holes with 3/8" dowel plugs glued in place, and sand them flush with the wood surfaces.

12. Sand the project lightly, and finish the wood with several coats of spray polyurethane.

Spice Rack

The warm colors of its contrasting woods and the protective retaining lip at each shelf's edge distinguish this spice rack from many others. The completed project can be mounted on a wall or rested on a counter top, and you'll find that its shelves are wide enough to accept boxes and tins as well as standard-sized jars of spices.

Materials List

Walnut and white oak is recommended for this project.

(4)	1/4" x 1" x 16"	Walnut retainer strips
(2)	3/4" x 2-1/2" x 16"	Oak frame base and crown
(2)	3/4" x 2-1/2" x 21"	Oak side rails
(3)	3/4" x 2-1/4" x 16"	Oak shelves
(1)	1/4" x 16-11/16" x 19-9/16"	Plywood back

Suggested Tools

3/8" drill
No. 8 pilot bit and countersink with stop collar
Router
1/4" roundover bit
1/2" straight bit
Tack hammer
Nail set
36" straightedge
No. 2 Phillips screwdriver
Jigsaw
Smooth file

Hardware & Supplies

No. 8 x 1" flathead wood screws
18-gauge x 3/4" brads
Spray lacquer

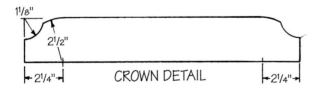

1¹/8"
2¹/2"
2¹/4"   CROWN DETAIL   2¹/4"

Construction Procedure

1. To create the decorative curve on the rack's crown, refer to the Crown Detail and to the following instructions. First, using two upper corners as centers, strike a 1-1/8" radius at each upper corner of one of the 2-1/2" x 16" oak pieces.

2. Then, on the same piece, measure 2-1/4" in from each end, and mark on the lower edge. Using these marked points as centers, strike two 2-1/2" radii to intersect with the 1-1/8" radii just made.

3. Use a jigsaw to cut the crown at the marked radii. Sand all its edges smooth.

4. Using a 1/4" roundover bit in the router, round the edges of all the radius cuts and the upper edge on one face. Then sand the crown well.

5. To round the upper outside corners of the 2-1/2" x 21" side rails, first measure and mark 1-7/8" down from one end of each rail. Measure 1-13/16" in from one edge, and mark to intersect the first line. Use that point on each piece to strike a 1-7/8" radius at the corner.

6. Cut both radii with a jigsaw, and sand the edges of both side rails smooth.

7. Use the 1/4" roundover bit to rout both the inside and outside of the front edges of both side rails. Sand both pieces of wood well.

8. With No. 8 x 1" flathead wood screws, fasten the side rails to the ends of the 2-1/2" x 16" oak frame base. Use the No. 8 pilot bit to drill holes 1-1/4" apart through the side rails' faces. Set the stop collar at 1-1/4".

9. Place the 2-1/2" x 16" crown at the top of the frame, flush with the sides' back edges; match the radius-cut ends. Secure the side rails to the crown as in Step 8, but space the screws vertically and 3/4" apart.

10. To locate positions for the 2-1/4" x 16" shelves, from the surface of the frame base, measure up and mark lines at the following distances on the inside of both side rails: 5-3/4", 11-1/4", and 16-3/4".

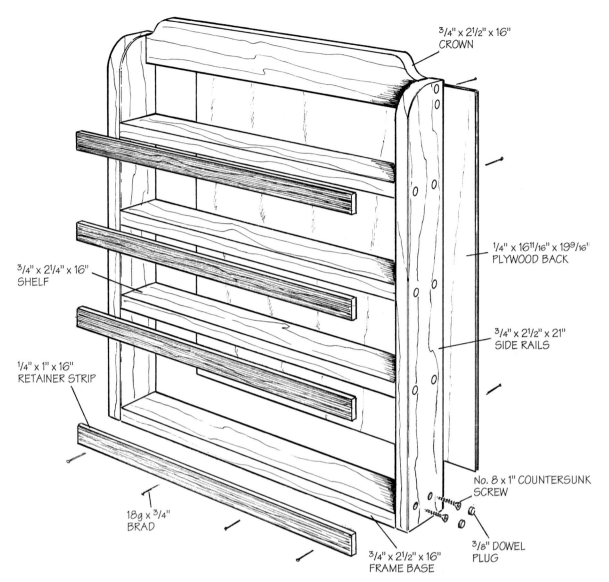

$^3/4" \times 2^1/2" \times 16"$
CROWN

$^1/4" \times 16^{11}/16" \times 19^9/16"$
PLYWOOD BACK

$^3/4" \times 2^1/4" \times 16"$
SHELF

$^3/4" \times 2^1/2" \times 21"$
SIDE RAILS

$^1/4" \times 1" \times 16"$
RETAINER STRIP

18g $\times$ $^3/4"$
BRAD

No. 8 $\times$ 1" COUNTERSUNK
SCREW

$^3/8"$ DOWEL
PLUG

$^3/4" \times 2^1/2" \times 16"$
FRAME BASE

11. Fasten the three shelves so that their bottom surfaces are even with the lines marked on the side rails; their front edges should be flush with the side rails' front edges. Fasten them in place using the same method as before, spacing the screws 1-1/4" apart.

12. Use the 1/4" roundover bit to round all the inside and outside edges on the front of the rack, except for the edge of the frame base.

13. Turn the assembled frame over, with its back facing up. Switch to a 1/2" straight bit, and rout the inside edges at the back of the assembled frame to make a dado 3/8" wide and 1/4" deep all around. Use a smooth-cut file to round the corners of the plywood back; then test-fit the back into the routed recess. Remove the plywood back; then sand its edges.

14. Round the long face edges of the 1" x 16" walnut retainer strips with the 1/4" roundover bit. Round the ends with a smoothing file.

15. Fasten the strips to the shelves' edges with 3/4" brads spaced 5" apart; counterset the brads. A 1/4" lip should protrude above the surface of each shelf.

16. Fasten the back to the frame in the same manner.

17. Plug all the screw holes with 3/8" dowel plugs glued in place. Sand them flush with the surface of the wood.

18. Finish the project with several coats of spray lacquer.

Paper Towel Stand

Some folks like their paper towels to hang horizontally. Other people prefer this vertical rack's design. We like both—which is why we've included both designs in this book. The small dowel that you see on this standing rack acts like an extra hand when you want to tear off a sheet; to pull a paper towel neatly off the roll, just draw it across the dowel.

Materials List

White or red oak is recommended for this project.

(1)   3/4" x 6" x 6"   Base plate
(1)   3/8" x 8-1/8"   Birch dowel
(1)   1-1/4" x 13-1/4"   Birch dowel

Suggested Tools

3/8" drill
3/8" drill bit
1-1/4" spade bit
No. 8 pilot bit and countersink with stop collar
Router
3/8" cove bit
Jigsaw
Compass
36" straightedge
No. 2 Phillips screwdriver

Hardware & Supplies

Yellow wood glue
No. 8 x 1-1/4" flathead wood screw
Spray lacquer

Construction Procedure

1. Locate the center of the 6" x 6" base plate by striking lines diagonally across its corners and across the length and width of the board.

2. Using the diagonal lines as centers for your compass, strike a 1-1/4" radius at each of the base plate's corners (see Base Plate Detail).

3. With a jigsaw, cut at the radius marks.

4. Using the spade bit, drill a 1-1/4" hole, 3/8" deep, in the center of the base plate.

5. Measure in 1" from one of the rounded corners, and mark a point at the diagonal line.

6. Using the 3/8" drill bit, bore a hole at this point to a depth of 3/8".

7. Rout the base plate's upper face edge, using a 3/8" cove bit in the router.

8. Sand the base and the two dowels.

9. Glue the 3/8" dowel into the small socket. Fasten the 1-1/4" dowel into its socket with a No. 8 x 1-1/4" flathead screw, inserted through the bottom of the base plate. Set the pilot bit's stop collar at 1-1/4".

10. Finish the project with several coats of spray lacquer.

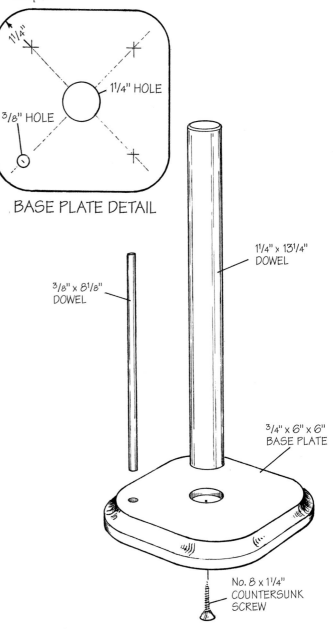

BASE PLATE DETAIL

1¼"

1¼" HOLE

3/8" HOLE

1¼" x 13¼" DOWEL

3/8" x 8⅛" DOWEL

3/4" x 6" x 6" BASE PLATE

No. 8 x 1¼" COUNTERSUNK SCREW

69

Paper Towel Holder

This holder is as easy to take apart as it is to put together. When you need to replace an empty roll of towels with a fresh one, just remove the two small pins, and slip the dowel rod out. If you prefer washable cotton towels to disposable paper ones, stitch together a loop of cotton material, and then slip the loop over the dowel.

Materials List

White pine is recommended for this project.

(1) 3/4" x 3-1/4" x 20-3/4"   Back and arms
(1) 3/4" x 13-1/4"   Birch dowel
(1) 1/4" x 5"   Birch dowel
                                 pins

Suggested Tools

36" straightedge
Try square
Compass
Jigsaw
Router
45° 7/16" chamfer bit
No. 2 Phillips screwdriver
3/8" drill
9/32" and 3/4" drill bits
No. 8 pilot bit and counterbore with stop collar

Hardware & Supplies

Yellow wood glue
No. 8 x 1-1/4" flathead wood screws
Spray lacquer

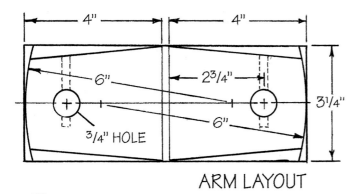

ARM LAYOUT

Construction Procedure

1. Strike a line directly down the center of the 3/4" x 3-1/4" x 20-3/4" piece, from end to end (see Arm Layout).

2. At this center line, measure and mark points 4" and 6" in from each end. Then, with a try square, mark lines across the wood at the 4" points.

3. With a compass, scribe a 6" radius at each end of the piece, using the 6" mark as a pivot point.

4. Measure 3/8" from each long edge, and strike lengthwise lines at these points. Draw diagonals from the points where the 3/8" lines cross the 6" radii to the edges where the 4" cross-lines are marked.

5. Use a jigsaw to cut the curved edges of the marked radii and the diagonal edges. To create the two arms, make two straight cuts on the lines marked at the 4" points; the remaining 12-3/4" section will serve as the rack's back.

6. Measure 2-3/4" from the square end of each 4" arm, and mark at the center line (see Arm Layout).

7. At these points, drill a 3/4" hole through each piece.

8. Using a 45° 7/16" chamfer bit in the router, chamfer all but the square-end edges of the two 4" arms, including the curved ends. Then center two chamfers, each 11" in length, in the face edges of the 12-3/4" back.

9. Sand all three pieces. Also sand down the 3/4" dowel so that it slips through the 3/4" holes in the arms.

10. Position the arms on the face of the back piece so that their exterior faces are flush with the back's ends. With a pilot bit and counterbore, drill holes 3/8" in from the back's ends (drilling from the back side) and into the square ends of the arms. Set the stop collar at a depth of 1-1/4".

11. Fasten the arms to the back with wood glue and No. 8 x 1-1/4" flathead wood screws.

12. When the glue has dried, chamfer the corners off the back piece with a router.

13. Center the dowel in its mounting holes. To create holes for the dowel pins, drill a 9/32" hole, 2" deep, through the top of each arm, 2-3/4" from the square ends. Both holes will penetrate the 3/4" dowel.

14. Cut the 1/4" dowel in half to make locking pins for the 3/4" dowel.

15. Remove the 3/4" dowel, sand all the wood lightly, and finish it with three or more coats of clear spray lacquer.

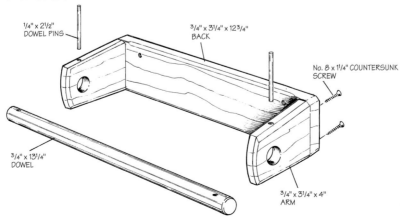

1/4" x 2½"
DOWEL PINS

3/4" x 3¼" x 12¾"
BACK

No. 8 x 1¼" COUNTERSUNK
SCREW

3/4" x 13¼"
DOWEL

3/4" x 3¼" x 4"
ARM

Spaghetti Measurer

How much spaghetti? The eternal question, and one we were never very good at answering. Either we'd end up eating pasta for three days in a row, or we'd have to disguise meager servings with oceans of sauce. The holes in this project's face put an end to our poor guesswork by measuring the spaghetti for us. Run the raw spaghetti through the appropriately sized hole, and your pasta-cooking won't be problematic any more.

Materials List

Walnut is recommended for this project.

   (1)   5/16" x 2-1/4" x 9-1/2"   Wood block

Suggested Tools

Jigsaw
3/8" drill
3/4", 1", 1-1/4", 1-1/2" drill bits
Compass
12" straightedge

Hardware & Supplies

Food-grade bowl finish

Construction Procedure

1. Measure and mark a 1-1/8" center line along the length of the wood block.

2. Using this line as a pivot point for your compass, mark a 1-1/8" radius at one end of the block and a 7/8" radius at the opposite end.

3. Define the measurer's outline by drawing straight lines to join the outer edges of one radius to the outer edges of the other.

4. Measuring from the end with the larger radius, make marks along the center line at 1-1/2", 3-1/2", 5-1/4", and 6-7/8" points.

5. Clamp the block, with a piece of scrap wood beneath it, to your work surface.

6. At the four marked points, drill 1-1/2", 1-1/4", 1", and 3/4" holes through the wood block, placing the largest hole at the end with the larger radius.

7. Use a jigsaw to cut along the project's outline.

8. Sand the measurer completely, including the hole edges.

9. Finish the wood with a food-grade bowl finish.

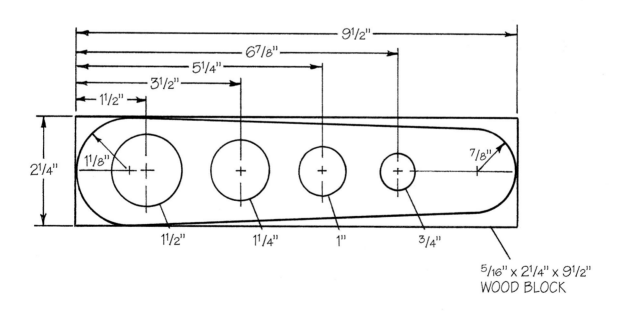

5/16" x 2 1/4" x 9 1/2"
WOOD BLOCK

Oven-Rack Pull

Oven mitts are wonderful creatures, but they don't protect your arms from heat when you try to retrieve a baking dish from deep inside the oven. Instead of plunging into the inferno to reach your evening meal, give this oven-rack pull a try. Just hook the instrument over one rung of the hot rack, and pull the shelf out toward you.

Materials List

White or red oak is recommended for this project.

(1)   5/16" x 2" x 11"   Handle

Suggested Tools

3/8" drill
3/4" drill bit
Coping saw
12" straightedge
Half-round bastard file

Hardware & Supplies

Masking tape
Food-grade bowl finish

Construction Procedure

1. The grid pattern in the illustration is scaled so that one square equals 1/2". Draw a 1/2"-block grid pattern on a piece of paper, and mark the outline of the handle and the hole placement as shown.

2. Cut out the paper template. Next, tape it to the 2" x 11" piece of stock, and then trace the handle's outline and hole center onto the wood.

3. After removing the template, drill the 3/4" hole where marked.

4. With a coping saw, cut the wooden stock to shape.

5. Use a half-round bastard file to take out the saw marks and to round the handle's edges. Sand the wood smooth.

6. Finish the project with several coats of food-grade bowl finish.

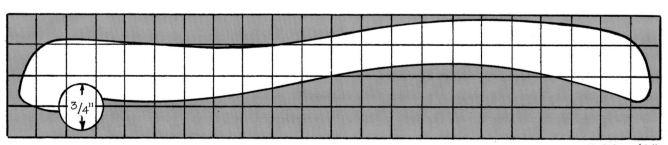

3/4"

1 SQ. = 1/2"

Bread Rack

If you wrap freshly baked bread while it's hot, trapped moisture will make it soggy. If you slice the loaf right away, steam will escape—steam that finishes the baking process. And if you move it straight from the pan to a counter top, condensation will make your bread look (and taste) like it's been standing in a puddle. Cool your bread on this distinctive rack instead. Air will circulate around the entire loaf, the crust will remain intact, and the texture will be irresistible.

Materials List

Black walnut is recommended for this project.

(2) 3/4" x 1-3/4" x 14"   Sides
(17) 1/4" x 8-5/8"   Birch dowels

Suggested Tools

Router
Jigsaw
3/8" drill
36" straightedge
Compass
1/4" drill bit with 1/4" stop collar
45° 7/16" chamfer bit

Hardware & Supplies

Waterproof wood glue
Food-grade bowl finish

Construction Procedure

1. Measure 1" in from each end of both 14" pieces, and mark on the sides and top edges.

2. To round the rack's ends, measure 2" in from each end of both pieces, and mark on the bottom edge of one face. From these 2" marks, strike a 2" radius across the face of each board, at each end (see Dowel Placement).

3. Measure up 1" from the bottom edge of each piece and mark a line lengthwise.

4. From the point where the previous 1" marks intersect the line drawn in Step 3, measure and mark points every 3/4" along each piece's lengthwise line so that there are seventeen marks all told (see Dowel Placement).

5. Using the 1/4" drill bit and a stop collar set to 3/8", drill 1/4" holes on the marked centers to a depth of 3/8". (Do not penetrate the opposite faces.) There should be a total of thirty-four holes altogether.

6. With a jigsaw, cut the marked radii on both ends of each piece.

7. Using the 7/16" chamfer bit in the router, chamfer all top and end edges of both pieces' face sides. (The face side is the side opposite the holes.) Sand the pieces smooth.

8. Glue the seventeen dowels into the set of sockets on one side piece, taking care not to overfill the holes with glue. Fasten the dowels into the second side piece in the same manner, starting at one end and working your way to the other. Clamp the sides firmly together, and set the rack on a flat surface while the glue dries.

9. Sand the project lightly. Apply food-grade bowl finish to the completed rack.

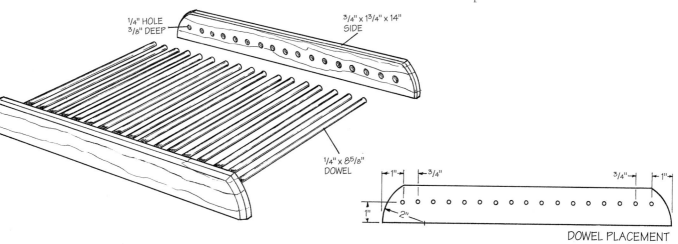

1/4" HOLE 3/8" DEEP

3/4" x 1³/4" x 14" SIDE

1/4" x 8⁵/8" DOWEL

1" 3/4"   3/4" 1"
1" 2"

DOWEL PLACEMENT

Stemware Rack

Storing your stemware in a kitchen cabinet has one major disadvantage; you can't show off your elegant crystal when it's hidden. This under-the-cupboard rack lets each lovely glass hang upside down—visible but out of harm's way. When you're ready to pour the wine, all you need to do is slip out the glasses.

Materials List

White or red oak is recommended for this project.

(5)	3/4" x 2-3/4" x 18"	Slats
(5)	1/4" x 3/4" x 18"	Strips
(2)	3/4" x 1-1/4" x 21-1/4"	Supports

Suggested Tools

Router
45° 7/16" chamfer bit
36" straightedge
Tack hammer
No. 2 Phillips screwdriver
3/8" drill
No. 8 pilot bit and counterbore with stop collar

Hardware & Supplies

Yellow wood glue
No. 8 x 1-1/4" flathead wood screws
18-gauge x 3/4" brads
Spray polyurethane

Construction Procedure

1. Using a 45° 7/16" chamfer bit in the router, chamfer the two edges on one face of each of the five 3/4" x 2-3/4" x 18" slats to a depth of 1/2".

2. Sand the slats, the strips, and the supports.

3. Fasten one 1/4" x 3/4" strip to the center of each slat's routed face, using glue and 18-gauge x 3/4" brads. Place the brads toward the ends and at the middle of the strips to avoid having them interfere with the wood screws which will secure the slats later.

4. Measure 2" in from each end of the slat and strip assemblies, and mark the strips at these points.

5. Measure 2-1/4" in from each end of the 21-1/4" supports, and mark the 3/4" edges. Then place the five slats, face down, on your work surface so that their edges are 1-1/8" apart. Lay the faces of the supports across the strips; the edge marks on the supports should line up with the outer edges of the end slats, and the supports' outer edges should, in turn, be in line with the 2" marks on each strip.

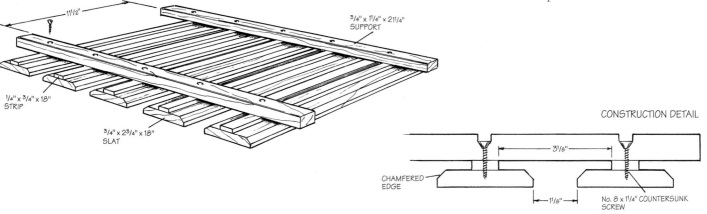

11 1/2"

3/4" x 1 1/4" x 21 1/4"
SUPPORT

1/4" x 3/4" x 18"
STRIP

3/4" x 2 3/4" x 18"
SLAT

CONSTRUCTION DETAIL

3 1/8"

CHAMFERED
EDGE

1 1/8"

No. 8 x 1 1/4" COUNTERSUNK
SCREW

6. At the points where the supports cross each strip, center a mark, and drill a pilot hole and counterbore. Set the stop collar at a depth of 1-1/4" to prevent the screws from penetrating the slat faces.

7. Fasten the supports to the back of the slats with No. 8 x 1-1/4" flathead wood screws.

8. Drill countersunk mounting holes for No. 8 screws, 1" in from the end of each support (or wherever is most appropriate for your type of installation).

9. Lightly sand the project. Then finish the wood with three or more coats of clear spray polyurethane.

Tiled Coasters

Because the tiles in these coasters can be personally selected to match any kitchen's color scheme, they make wonderful presents for friends and family. The finished pieces nest in a convenient stand, one that's small enough to fit on a windowsill but appealing enough to display almost anywhere in the house.

Materials List

White pine is recommended for this project.

(1)	3/8" x 3-3/4" x 15-1/2"	Coaster bases
(1)	3/8" x 4-3/4" x 4-3/4"	Base
(1)	1/4" x 12"	Birch dowel pins
(4)	3" x 3"	Ceramic tiles

Suggested Tools

Table saw
3/8" drill
1/4" drill bit
Router
1/4" straight bit
1/2" chisel
Coping saw
Try square
C-clamp
12" straightedge

Hardware & Supplies

Yellow wood glue
Latex cement adhesive
Masking tape
Spray lacquer

Construction Procedure

1. Measure 3/8" from the end of the 15-1/2" board, and using a try square, strike a line across its width.

2. Measure 3" from the line, and strike a second line across the board's width. Then strike a third line 3/8" from the second, and a fourth line 1/8" from the third. (The 1/8" line allows for saw kerf when the coaster bases are cut.)

3. Repeat the procedure three more times to mark cutting lines for a total of four 3-3/4"-square coaster bases.

4. Now measure in 3/8" from each long edge, and strike lines lengthwise down the board. Note that these two lines, along with the lines drawn earlier, define the routed areas in which tiles will eventually be set.

5. Clamp the piece to a bench, and using the straight bit in the router, remove the 3"-square marked

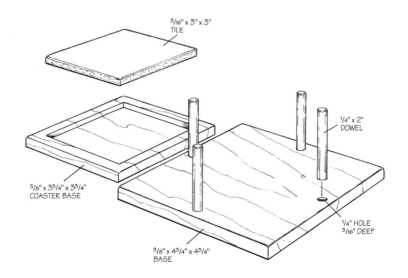

3/16" x 3" x 3"
TILE

1/4" x 2"
DOWEL

3/8" x 3 3/4" x 3 3/4"
COASTER BASE

1/4" HOLE
3/16" DEEP

3/8" x 4 3/4" x 4 3/4"
BASE

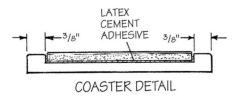

LATEX CEMENT ADHESIVE

3/8"   3/8"

COASTER DETAIL

centers to a depth of 3/16" (or to the specific thickness of your purchased tiles). A 3/8" border should remain all around each tile bed.

6. Cut the piece into four squares along the marked 1/8" lines.

7. Clean and square the corners of the routed areas with a chisel, and sand the four pieces lightly.

8. Cover the routed area with masking tape, and finish the wood with several coats of spray lacquer.

9. After removing the tape, cement the tiles into their beds with the latex adhesive. Use a damp sponge to clean up any excess cement.

10. Using the straightedge and square, mark two center lines across and along the face of the 4-3/4" base.

11. On the center lines, measure and mark points 5/16" in from each edge.

12. At each mark, drill a 1/4" hole to a depth of 3/16"

13. With a coping saw, cut four 2" lengths from the 12" dowel.

14. Glue the dowels into the four holes in the base, and sand the assembled base lightly.

15. Finish the base with several coats of spray lacquer.

Candlesticks

Even a kitchen table is sometimes graced with a fancy meal, and what would a fancy meal be without candles? These handsome candlesticks are nothing more than blocks of wood with a pleasant design cut into their sides. One warning, however: use only dripless candles. If you don't, you may be spending more time than you'd like carving melted wax out of the decorative grooves!

Materials List

Walnut is recommended for this project.

(1)	1-7/8" x 1-7/8" x 6-1/4"	Tall holder
(1)	1-7/8" x 1-7/8" x 5"	Short holder

Suggested Tools

Table saw
3/8" drill
7/8" drill bit
12" straightedge

Hardware & Supplies

Spray lacquer

Construction Procedure

1. On two opposing sides of each block, measure and mark lines at the following distances from the blocks' top ends: 1/2", 7/8", and 1-1/4". (Refer to the Kerf Detail before marking all lines.)

2. Set the table saw to cut at a 1/8" depth. Pass the blocks through the saw, cutting to the same side of each line. Each block should have two sets of cuts when you're through.

3. Next, measure over 5/16" from the right edge, and strike a line. Repeat at all the right-hand edges on both blocks.

4. Cut a 1/8"-deep saw kerf to the left of each of these lines.

5. Measure and mark a line 5/8" from the right edge of the sides without the crosscuts. Cut a 1/8"-deep saw kerf to the left of each of these lines, for a total of two cuts per block.

6. On each block, mark the center of the end closest to the crosscuts.

7. Use a 7/8" drill bit to bore a 7/8"-deep hole into each block's end at the marked points.

8. Clean the grooves with a folded piece of sandpaper. Sand the blocks' faces lightly, and finish the wood with several coats of spray lacquer.

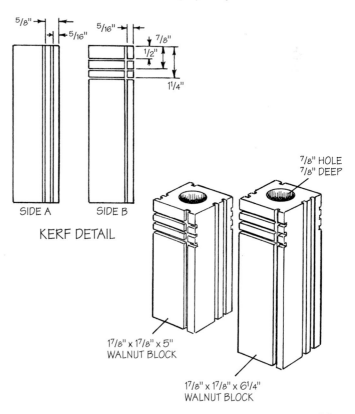

Napkin Holders

If you associate paper napkins with a lack of style, it's time to change your perspective. After all, it's the napkin holder, not the napkin itself, that draws attention. As well as doing their jobs, these two distinctive projects will add a touch of class to any dining occasion, from picnics to formal indoor luncheons.

Napkin Holder #1

Materials List

Walnut and red or white oak are recommended for this project.

(2)	3/4" x 5-1/4" x 6"	Walnut sides
(1)	3/4" x 3-5/8" x 8-1/2"	Oak base
(1)	1/4", 3/8", 3/4"	Birch dowel plugs

Suggested Tools

3/8" drill
1/4", 3/8", 3/4" drill bits
Tack hammer
Jigsaw
Router
45° 7/16" chamfer bit
Compass

Hardware & Supplies

Yellow wood glue
16-gauge x 1" brads
Spray lacquer

Construction Procedure

1. On each 6" side piece, first locate the centers. Then mark a straight line across the width and height (see Side Detail).

2. Make two half-circle patterns by striking a 6" and a 9-7/8" radius across two pieces of cardboard. Cut out the patterns with a razor.

3. Transfer the 9-7/8" radius to one 6" edge of each piece, and repeat the process at the opposite 6" edge, but this time allow the pattern board to overlap the wood by 1/16" to create a flat edge at each side piece's bottom.

4. Mark the center of what will be the flat edge on both pieces by continuing the center line from the face of each piece across its edge.

5. On each flat edge, measure 3/8" to each side of the center mark. Then drill a 1/4" hole, 3/8" deep at each of these locations.

6. Transfer the 6" radius to both 5-1/4" edges of each piece.

7. Place each piece flat on a level surface, with its flat edge at the bottom. Next, on both pieces, strike lines 1-3/4" to the left of the vertical center lines. Measuring from the apex of the top curve, mark points 1-1/8" and 2" down along this line on each piece (see Side Detail).

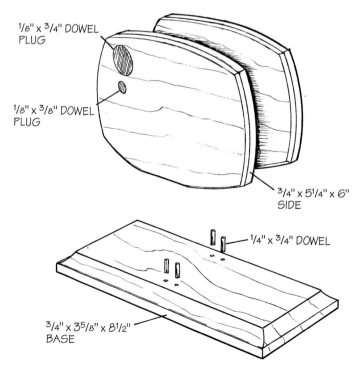

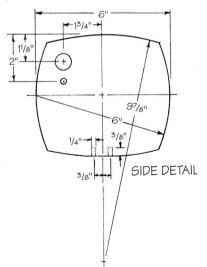

SIDE DETAIL

8. At each of the 1-1/8" points, drill a 3/4" hole to a depth of 1/8".

9. At the 2" points, drill 3/8" holes to a depth of 1/8".

10. Plug the four holes with 1/8" sections of corresponding dowel material, using glue to fasten the plugs. Sand the plugs smooth.

11. Use 1" brads to tack the two side pieces together, with the dowel plugs facing outward and in opposite corners. Place the brads in the corners, outside the marked radius lines.

12. With a jigsaw, match-cut the pieces on the marked lines. Sand the cut edges once the pieces are separated.

13. Use a 7/16" chamfer bit in the router to chamfer both sides of all edges. Sand both pieces.

14. Find the center of the base, and mark a line across its 3-5/8" width. Then strike two parallel lines 3/8" in from each long edge.

15. From the two points at which the three lines intersect, measure and mark points 3/8" to each side of the center line. Drill a 1/4" hole, 3/8" deep, at each of these four points.

16. Chamfer the upper edge of the base to a 3/8" width. If you wish, you may also chamfer the lower edge to a 1/8" width. Sand the base completely.

17. Cut four 1/4" dowels to 3/4" in length.

18. Glue the dowels to the base; then glue the sides onto the dowels.

19. Finish the project with several coats of spray lacquer.

Napkin Holder #2

Materials List

Cypress is recommended for this project.

(1)	3/4" x 5-5/8" x 8-1/2"	Upper base
(1)	3/4" x 4-3/4" x 7-1/2"	Lower base
(2)	3/4" x 1" x 7-1/2"	Side rails
(4)	1/4" x 5-1/4"	Acrylic rods
(4)	1/4" x 5-7/8"	Acrylic rods
(2)	1/4" x 6-1/2"	Acrylic rods

Suggested Tools

3/8" drill
1/4" drill bit
No. 8 pilot bit and countersink with stop collar
Router
3/8" roundover bit
45° 7/16" chamfer bit
3/8" cove bit
12" straightedge
No. 2 Phillips screwdriver
Try square

Hardware & Supplies

Household cement
No. 8 x 1" flathead wood screws
Spray lacquer

Construction Procedure

1. To locate holes for the acrylic rods, measure 1" from each long edge of the 5-5/8" x 8-1/2" upper base, and strike two lengthwise lines (see Rod Placement).

2. Measure 1-3/8" from each of the base's ends, and make marks at the 1" lines. Repeat at 3-5/8" and 4-1/4".

3. Drill 1/4" holes, 3/8" deep, at each of the ten marked points.

4. On the drilled face, use a 45° chamfer bit to rout all four edges. On the bottom face, round all four edges with a 3/8" roundover bit.

5. Rout all four edges on one face of the 4-3/4" x 7-1/2" lower base, using a 3/8" cove bit.

6. Center the lower base, with its routed side down, on the bottom of the upper base. Fasten the two pieces from the bottom of the lower base with No. 8 x 1" flathead wood screws placed 3" apart. Use a No. 8 pilot bit to make the holes, setting the stop collar at 1".

7. To locate holes for the acrylic rods on the 3/4" x 1" side rails, on the 3/4" face of each one, mark a line down the center. Measure 1", 3-1/8", and 3-3/4" from both ends of each rail, and make marks at the line.

8. At these marks, drill 1/4" holes through both rails.

9. Sand the wooden components, and finish them with several coats of spray lacquer.

10. Slip the four 5-1/4" acrylic rods through the end-most holes of both rails; then fit and cement them into the holes in the upper base. Adjust each rail so that its lower edge is 2-1/2" above the upper base's surface.

11. Slip the four 5-7/8" rods into the intermediate set of holes, and cement them in place.

12. Slip the two 6-1/2" rods into the remaining two center holes, and cement them in place. Use the cement sparingly so that none is forced from the holes.

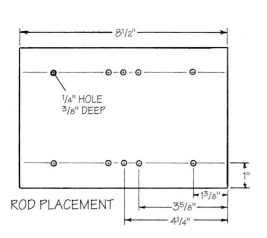

8¹⁄₂"

¹⁄₄" HOLE
³⁄₈" DEEP

ROD PLACEMENT

1"

1³⁄₈"

3⁵⁄₈"

4¹⁄₄"

NAPKIN HOLDER #2

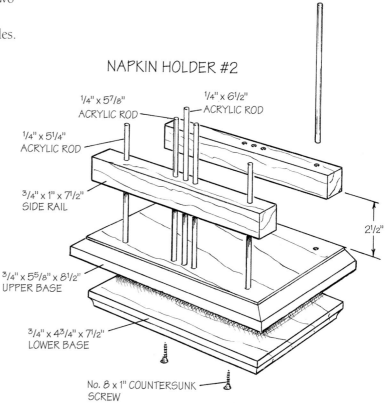

¹⁄₄" x 5⁷⁄₈"
ACRYLIC ROD

¹⁄₄" x 6¹⁄₂"
ACRYLIC ROD

¹⁄₄" x 5¹⁄₄"
ACRYLIC ROD

³⁄₄" x 1" x 7¹⁄₂"
SIDE RAIL

³⁄₄" x 5⁵⁄₈" x 8¹⁄₂"
UPPER BASE

³⁄₄" x 4³⁄₄" x 7¹⁄₂"
LOWER BASE

2¹⁄₂"

No. 8 x 1" COUNTERSUNK
SCREW

Wine Rack

As well as displaying your wine collection, a good wine rack protects it, too. How? By holding each bottle at a slight angle so that its cork is kept damp. Dry corks shrink; when they do, air can enter the bottle and damage its contents. This handsome project will fit comfortably under any standard cabinet or on a pantry shelf.

Materials List

Walnut and maple are recommended for this project.

(1)	3/4" x 2-3/4" x 73"	Maple racks
(2)	3/4" x 10" x 12-1/4"	Maple sides
(1)	1/4" x 3/4" x 102"	Walnut insets
(1)	3/4" x 2-3/4" x 18"	Scrap wood

Suggested Tools

3/8" drill
No. 8 pilot bit and countersink with stop collar
Router
1/2" straight bit
No. 2 Phillips screwdriver
Compass
36" straightedge
Palm sander
Jigsaw

Hardware & Supplies

Yellow wood glue
No. 8 x 1" flathead wood screws
3/8" dowel plugs
Spray lacquer

Construction Procedure

1. Measure 3/4" from one long edge of the 73" maple board, and strike a line lengthwise. Measure 1-1/2" from the same edge, and strike a second line parallel to the first.

2. Using the 1/2" straight bit in the router, cut a dado 3/4" wide and 1/4" deep between the marked lines.

3. Cut a 1/4" x 3/4" x 73" strip of walnut, and glue it into the dado just completed.

4. Cut the 2-3/4" x 73" maple board into four 18" rack pieces. Also cut a piece of 3/4" scrap wood to 2-3/4" x 18".

5. Lay one edge of the scrap piece next to the edge of a rack piece, with the ends flush and the rack's walnut inset facing out. (See the Rack Detail, in which the scrap piece rests above the rack itself). Measure 1" up from the inside edge of the scrap piece, and strike a line lengthwise. Then measure 2-11/16" and 6-7/8" in from each end of the scrap, and mark points across this line.

6. Strike a 1-3/4" radius across the rack's face from each of these four points. Repeat with the remaining three rack pieces.

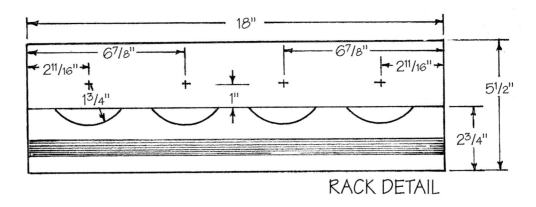

RACK DETAIL

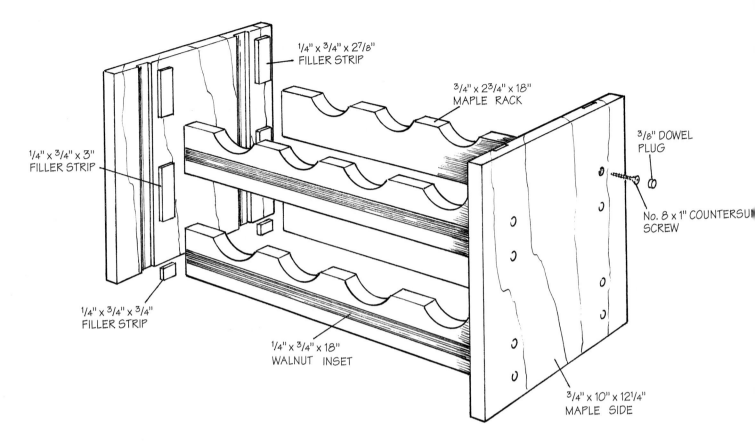

1/4" x 3/4" x 2 7/8"
FILLER STRIP

3/4" x 2 3/4" x 18"
MAPLE RACK

3/8" DOWEL
PLUG

No. 8 x 1" COUNTERSU
SCREW

1/4" x 3/4" x 3"
FILLER STRIP

1/4" x 3/4" x 3/4"
FILLER STRIP

1/4" x 3/4" x 18"
WALNUT INSET

3/4" x 10" x 12 1/4"
MAPLE SIDE

7. With a jigsaw, cut along the radius lines on all four rack pieces. Sand their edges and faces.

8. To locate the filler strip channels in the wine rack's sides, measure 1-1/2" and 2-1/4" from each long edge of the two 10" x 12-1/4" maple side pieces. Strike a lengthwise line at each point.

9. Use a 1/2" straight bit to rout a dado 3/4" wide and 1/4" deep at each of these four marked channels.

10. Cut the remaining walnut strip into twelve pieces: four 3/4" long, four 3" long, and four 2-7/8" long.

11. Glue the 3/4"-long walnut filler strips into the dadoes at the bottom end of each 10" x 12-1/4" side piece; glue the 2-7/8"-long strips into the dadoes at the top end. The end of each filler strip should be flush with the ends of the side pieces. Allow eight hours for the glue to dry.

12. Fasten the maple sides to the ends of the racks so that the radii on each rack are facing in the direction of the 2-7/8" filler strips. Butt the racks' outer edges against the walnut strips so that there's a 3" space between each upper and lower rack. Use the No. 8 pilot bit to drill holes 1-1/4" apart, through the sides and into the rack's ends; set the stop collar at 1-1/4". Secure the joints with No. 8 x 1" flathead screws.

13. Plug the screw holes with 3/8" dowel plugs glued in place. Sand the plugs flush with the wood's surface.

14. Glue the remaining four 3"-long walnut strips into the exposed dadoes between the racks. Adjust the strips' lengths as necessary to make them fit.

15. Sand the project lightly, and finish the wood with several coats of spray lacquer.

16. Place your wine bottles in the racks so that their necks tilt slightly downward.

A Very Large Dinner Bell

Why should a dinner bell be discreet? This one will let you summon your children from three blocks away, paralyze night prowlers, and punish howling dogs, as well as announce that supper is served. We tend to be a bit inhibited, so our gong is made of copper and doesn't ring very loudly, but a stainless steel pan will let you put the bells of Notre Dame to shame.

Materials List

Walnut is recommended for this project.

(2)	3/4" x 2-1/4" x 20"	Uprights
(1)	3/4" x 4" x 13"	Upper base plate
(1)	5/8" x 5" x 14-1/8"	Lower base plate
(2)	3/4" x 13-1/2"	Birch dowels
(1)	1" x 14-1/2"	Birch dowel
(1)	3/8" x 9-1/2"	Birch dowel mallet handle

Suggested Tools

3/8" drill
No. 8 pilot bit and countersink with stop collar
1/16", 1/8", and 3/8" drill bits
3/4" and 1" spade bits
Jigsaw
Router
45° 7/16" chamfer bit
36" straightedge
Compass
Try square
No. 2 Phillips screwdriver
Tack hammer

Hardware & Supplies

No. 8 x 1" flathead wood screws
No. 8 x 1-1/4" flathead wood screws
16-gauge x 1-1/4" brads
9-gauge x 1-9/16" screw eyes (2)
14-gauge x 1-5/16" screw hook
1-1/4"-diameter wooden ball
Spray lacquer

Construction Procedure

1. Locate the center of the 2-1/4" width of each 20" upright piece, and strike a line lengthwise at that point. Mark a 2" radius from the center line on one end of each piece (see Upright Detail).

2. Measure 1-1/4" and 2-5/8" down from the same end, and mark on the center line. On the opposite end of each piece, measure up 1-3/8" and mark.

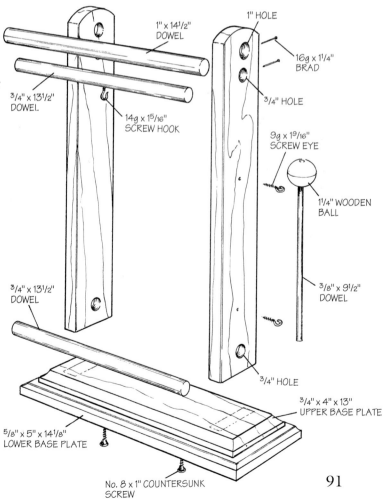

3. Using sharp spade bits, drill 1" holes on the two 1-1/4" marks and 3/4" holes on the 2-5/8" and 1-3/8" marks.

4. Cut each upright's radius-marked ends with a jigsaw.

5. To locate positions for the uprights on the 4" x 13" upper base plate, measure 1-1/4" in from each end, and mark across the piece. Then measure 2" in from each end, and make a second set of marks. Strike lines 7/8" from the plate's edges to cross these marks.

6. Use a chamfer bit to rout all the upper edges of the upper base plate to a depth of 7/8". Sand the plate when the routing has been completed.

7. Measure 9/16" in from each end of the 5" x 14-1/8" lower base plate, and strike lines across the width of the piece. Measure 1/2" in from the edges, and strike lengthwise lines. The resulting marked rectangle will establish the placement of the upper base plate.

8. With the chamfer bit, rout the lower base plate's upper edges to a depth of 1/8". Sand the plate thoroughly.

9. Slip the cut dowels through the appropriate holes in the uprights, and center the uprights so that they align with the guide marks on the upper base plate. To secure the dowels, drive and set 16-gauge x 1-1/4" brads through one edge of each upright. (Pre-drill the holes with a 1/16" bit to prevent the wood from splitting.)

10. Mount the assembled uprights to the upper base plate with No. 8 x 1-1/4" flathead screws driven from the plate's bottom. Use a No. 8 pilot bit to drill the holes, and set the stop collar at 1-1/4". (Note that these screws are not visible in the illustration.)

11. Mount the upper base plate to the lower base plate with No. 8 x 1" screws driven from the bottom of the lower base plate. Set the stop collar at 1".

12. Drill a 3/8" hole in the 1-1/4" wooden ball; then glue the 3/8" dowel handle into it.

13. From the upper base plate's surface, measure up 4" and 11", and mark these points on one outer face of one upright. Drill 1/8" holes at each point, being careful not to penetrate the upright's opposite face. Fasten the two screw eyes into these pre-drilled holes, aligning the openings in the two eyes. These will hold the mallet handle.

14. Locate the center of the upper 3/4" dowel, and drill a 1/16" hole into its bottom face. Thread the 1-5/16" screw hook into the hole; the gong will hang from this hook.

15. Sand the project lightly. Then finish it with several coats of spray lacquer.

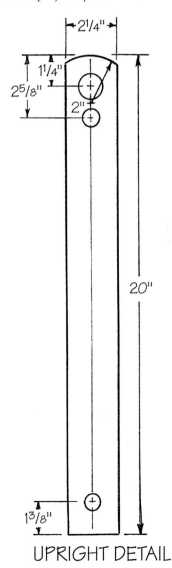

UPRIGHT DETAIL

Tiled Cheese Board

Based on a traditional cutting-board design, this cheese board is light enough to pass around among your guests, but large enough to hold the knife and crackers too! Its hand-selected tile gives it a special flair. Choose a tile color and pattern that please you—ones that will complement your kitchen or dining-room decor.

Materials List

Birch and cherry are recommended for this project.

(2)	3/4" x 3-3/16" x 18"	Birch sides
(1)	3/4" x 3-3/4" x 18"	Cherry center
(1)	6" x 8"	Ceramic tile

Suggested Tools

Router
1/4" straight bit
3/8" roundover bit
Jigsaw
Try square
36" straightedge
Pipe clamps
Compass
Sander

Hardware & Supplies

Waterproof wood glue
Latex cement adhesive
Masking tape
Food-grade bowl finish

Construction Procedure

1. Spread glue evenly along the edges of each piece, and clamp the sections together with the cherry wood in the center. Use the square or straightedge to check for a level surface before allowing the glue to dry overnight.

2. If necessary, use a table saw to trim the piece to 10" x 18" dimensions. At the center of the board's width, strike a center line lengthwise.

3. Measure in 6-1/2" from one end, and mark a point on the center line. Then, from this point, strike a 6-1/2" radius at the board's end (see Board Layout).

4. On the same end, using the corners as centers, mark two 2" radii that intersect with the arc just made.

5. Mark lines across the board, 3" and 9" from this end.

6. Measure 4" to each side of the center line previously marked, and strike two parallel lines that intersect with the two lines made in Step 5.

7. Using a straight bit in the router, remove the material within the marked 6" x 8" rectangle to a depth of 1/4". Start in the center, and work out toward the edges to prevent the router base from slipping out of square with the wood's surface.

8. On the opposite 10" end, measure in 2" from the sides and end of the board, and mark the two points.

9. Strike a 2" radius at each of these points to form the rounded board's corners.

10. With a jigsaw, cut the board to the shape marked.

11. Use a 3/8" roundover bit in the router to round both sides of all edges.

12. After sanding the wood, cover the tile bed with masking tape.

13. Finish the wood with several coats of food-grade bowl finish.

14. Remove the masking tape, and glue the tile in place with latex cement adhesive. Use a damp cloth to remove any excess glue.

Salad Fork & Spoon

This unique fork and spoon set isn't as difficult to create as you might think; we've provided patterns that are easily transferred. If you'd rather invent your own design, just make a few sketches and transfer your favorites to the utensil stock. The basic construction process won't vary much, no matter which design you select.

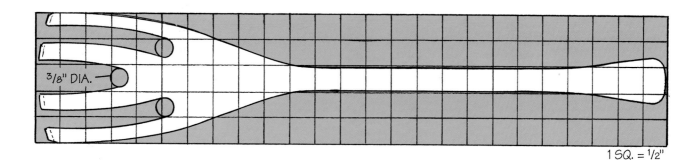

3/8" DIA.

1 SQ. = 1/2"

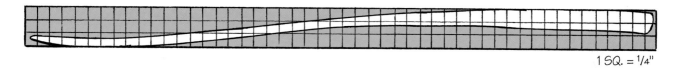

1 SQ. = 1/4"

Materials List

Cherry is recommended for this project.

(2) 3/4" x 2-1/2" x 12-1/2" Utensils

Suggested Tools

3/8" drill
3/8" drill bit
Coping saw
12" straightedge
C-clamp
3/8" round file
Half-round bastard file

Hardware & Supplies

Masking tape
Food-grade bowl finish

Construction Procedure

1. The grid patterns in the illustrations are scaled so that one square equals 1/2". Draw two 1/2"-block grid patterns on a piece of paper. On one, mark the face outline of the fork and the tang slots as shown. On the other, mark the edge outline.

2. Cut out the paper face template, and tape it to one of the 2-1/2" x 12-1/2" pieces of stock. Trace it, including the tang slots, onto the wood. Remove it and tape it to the second piece of stock; this time, to create the spoon pattern, eliminate the fork slots, and trace only the full shape of the head and handle.

3. On both pieces of stock, use a coping saw to cut out the face shape of the spoon; do not try to cut the fork slots yet.

4. To cut the slots in the fork, first drill three 3/8" holes at the inner end of the tang slots; then cut the slots themselves.

5. Cut out the paper edge template, and tape it to the edge of one utensil. Trace it onto the wood. Then remove the pattern, place it on the second utensil, and trace again.

6. Clamp each utensil down, and carefully cut the edge (or side-view) shape.

7. Use a half-round bastard file to remove the saw marks and round the edges of each utensil. Sand both pieces smooth afterwards.

8. Finish both the fork and the spoon with several coats of a food-grade bowl finish.

Not-So-Lazy Susan

A Lazy Susan isn't—lazy, that is. In fact, this traditional kitchen project has much to recommend it. It's a time-saver, it's efficient, and it consolidates counter-top clutter. You can also use this attractive piece as a rotating platter, right on the kitchen or dining room table.

Materials List

White oak is recommended for this project.

(1) 3/4" x 15-1/2" x 15-1/2"   Turntable
(1) 3/4" x 11" x 19"   Base plate

Suggested Tools

Pipe clamps
Jigsaw
3/8" drill
Drill bit to fit kit hardware
3/4" spade bit
No. 2 Phillips screwdriver
Router
3/8" roundover bit
Compass
36" straightedge

Hardware & Supplies

Lazy Susan hardware kit
Yellow wood glue
Spray lacquer

Construction Procedure

1. Glue up available 3/4" stock to 15-1/2" x 15-1/2" dimensions. Spread glue evenly along the surfaces to be joined, and clamp the pieces squarely and evenly. Allow the glue to dry overnight, and then sand the surfaces level.

2. From the center of this piece, strike a circle with a 7-1/2" radius. Use a jigsaw to cut the 15"-diameter turntable from the board.

3. Use a 3/8" roundover bit to round all the turntable's edges, and then sand it well.

4. Glue up 3/4" stock to 11" x 19" dimensions, using the same technique as before. Once the glue has dried, use the jigsaw to cut the 10-1/4" x 18-3/4" base plate.

5. Locate the center of the base plate by striking center lines across its width and length.

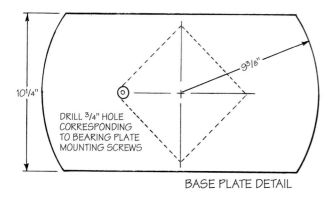

10¼"

9³∕₈"

DRILL ³⁄₄" HOLE
CORRESPONDING
TO BEARING PLATE
MOUNTING SCREWS

BASE PLATE DETAIL

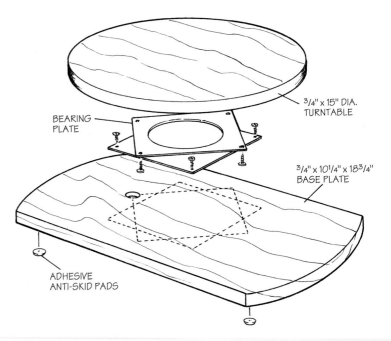

³⁄₄" x 15" DIA.
TURNTABLE

BEARING
PLATE

³⁄₄" x 10¼" x 18³⁄₄"
BASE PLATE

ADHESIVE
ANTI-SKID PADS

6. From this center point, strike a 9-3/8" radius on each end of the base plate (see Base Plate Detail). Use a jigsaw to cut along the radius lines.

7. With a 3/8" roundover bit, round the edges on both faces of the base plate, and then sand it well.

8. Center the Lazy Susan hardware on both the turntable and the base plate, and mark. Temporarily mount the hardware, following instructions provided in the purchased kit. Be sure to drill a 3/4" access hole through the base plate where indicated so that the turntable bearing plate can be fastened from below.

9. Remove the hardware, and finish the wood with several coats of spray lacquer. Reassemble the kit.

Spaghetti Spoon

The only thing more annoying than cooking too much or too little spaghetti is trying to serve the spaghetti you cook. If you've ever plastered a table with strands of the slippery stuff as you tried to transfer a single serving from pot to plate, you'll love this serving spoon. Plunge it into the bowl, give it a twist, and lift it out; the small dowels will be wrapped with just the right amount of pasta.

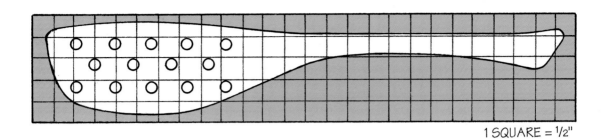

1 SQUARE = 1/2"

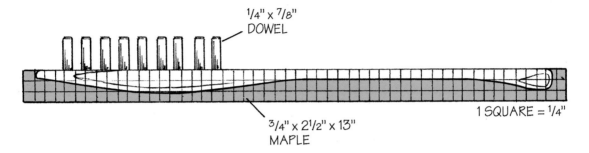

1/4" x 7/8"
DOWEL

1 SQUARE = 1/4"

3/4" x 2-1/2" x 13"
MAPLE

Materials List

Maple is recommended for this project.

(1)   3/4" x 2-1/2" x 13"   Handle
(1)   1/4" x 36"   Birch dowel

Suggested Tools

3/8" drill
1/4" drill bit
C-clamp
Coping saw
12" straightedge
Half-round bastard file

Hardware & Supplies

Waterproof wood glue
Masking tape
Food-grade bowl finish

Construction Procedure

1. The illustrated grid patterns are scaled so that one square equals 1/2". Draw both grid patterns on a piece of paper; mark the face outline of the spoon and the hole placement on one pattern and the edge outline on the other.

2. Cut out the paper face template, tape it onto the 2-1/2" x 13" wood stock, and trace its outline. Mark the centers of each hole by pressing any sharp instrument through the center of the template's holes.

3. Drill the fourteen 1/4" holes to a depth of 1/4".

4. With a coping saw, cut out the face shape of the spoon.

5. Cut out the paper edge template, and trace it onto the edge of the spoon stock.

6. Clamp the spoon in place, and carefully cut the edge (or side-view) shape.

7. Use a half-round bastard file to take out the saw marks and to round the edges of the spoon. Sand the wood smooth afterwards.

8. Use the coping saw to cut fourteen 7/8" lengths of dowel.

9. Glue the dowels into their sockets with waterproof wood glue. Wipe up any excess glue from the surface of the wood immediately.

10. Dress the spoon with several coats of a food-grade bowl finish.

Meat Platter

If you've ever tried to carve a succulent ham or roast on a slippery platter, you'll understand why we designed this wooden carving surface! A knife won't harm it, juice collects in its grooves instead of on the tablecloth, and the meat doesn't move until it's meant to!

Materials List

Cherry is recommended for this project.

(3)   3/4" x 5" x 19"   Platter sections

Suggested Tools

Table saw
Jigsaw
36" straightedge
Try square
Pipe clamps (4)
Router
1/2" core box bit
3/8" roundover bit
Router guide

Hardware & Supplies

Waterproof wood glue
Food-grade bowl finish

Construction Procedure

1. Examine the long edges of each board; these should be straight and square. If they aren't, run each section through the table saw to dress its edge surfaces. Trial-fit the three sections together.

2. Spread glue evenly along the joining edge surfaces. Clamp the pieces together, using the square or straightedge to be sure that the sections are level. Wipe off any excess glue immediately, and allow the assembly to dry overnight.

3. Cut the glued-up board to 12" x 18" dimensions. Sand both sides level.

4. On both ends, measure and mark points 2-1/2" in from the long edges. Then, on both edges, measure 2" in from the short ends and make a second set of marks (see Groove Layout). Strike a diagonal line between the two points at each corner.

GROOVE LAYOUT

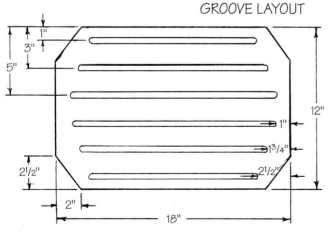

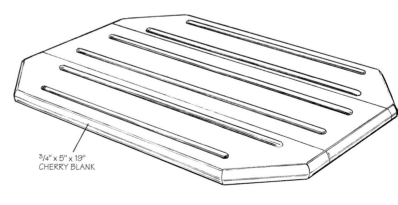

3/4" x 5" x 19"
CHERRY BLANK

5. Measure in 1" from each long edge, and mark the face of the board along its length. Repeat this procedure at 3" and 5" distances to create six parallel lines.

6. To create stop points for your router, measure in from each short edge as follows: At the 1" lines, mark at 2-1/2"; at the 3" lines, mark at 1-3/4"; at the 5" lines, mark at 1".

7. Install a 1/2" core box bit and the router guide into the router. Each time you rout a marked slot, set the guide so that the marked lines represent the slot

centers. Adjust the depth of cut to 1/8", and make at least two passes between the stop points for each slot.

8. With a jigsaw, cut along the marked corner lines. Sand the edges.

9. Use a 3/8" roundover bit in the router to round all the edges on the platter's top and bottom.

10. Sand the project thoroughly, and then apply several coats of a food-grade bowl finish to it.

Tiled Trivets

Like the tiled coasters, these trivets are not only functional but can also serve to accent the colors and mood of your kitchen or dining room. They're easy to make (and to alter), too. The tile is glued into a routed rectangle and is raised above the surrounding base so that you'll never scorch the wood when you rest a steaming kettle or casserole on the project's surface.

Materials List

White or red oak is recommended for this project.

(1)	1/2" x 7-3/8" x 19"	Base plate
(2)	6" x 8"	Ceramic tiles
	(Actual dimensions 5-7/8" x 7-7/8")	

Suggested Tools

Router
Table saw
36" straightedge
1/2" chisel
1-1/4" putty knife
1/4" straight bit
3/8" cove bit

Hardware & Supplies

Latex cement adhesive
Masking tape
Spray lacquer

Hint: *Be sure to purchase a heat-resistant adhesive!*

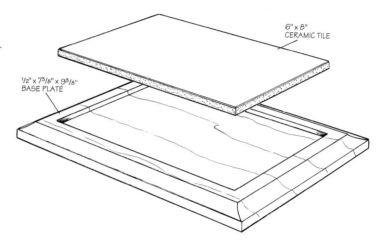

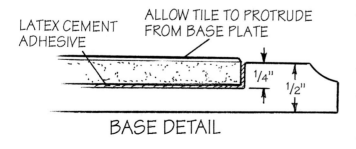

LATEX CEMENT ADHESIVE

ALLOW TILE TO PROTRUDE FROM BASE PLATE

1/4"   1/2"

BASE DETAIL

Construction Procedure

1. This project yields two trivets. Measure the actual size of your tiles to be sure that the wooden base will be large enough to accommodate them. For tiles measuring 5-7/8" x 7-7/8", the wood border around each tile should be at least 3/4".

2. Strike a line across the center of the 19" board. To establish the saw kerf, mark lines 1/16" to each side of this center line. Lay the tiles on top of the wood, and check to see that the borders will be sufficient. Remember to allow 1-5/8" between the two tiles (two 3/4" borders plus 1/8" extra to allow for the saw kerf). Measure 3/4" out from the other edges of each tile and mark lines. (You may alter this dimension if you'd prefer a tile with wider borders.)

3. If the edges of the wood need to be trimmed, make the cuts on a table saw. Do not cut the kerf line between the tiles yet; you'll need the entire base to support your router.

4. Measure 3/4" in from the marked edges, and mark across and down the length of the board. Measure 3/4" to each side of the kerf lines, and mark across the board.

5. Measure the thickness of your tiles; then set the router depth 1/16" less than that dimension. This 1/16" allowance, plus the thickness of the cement, will raise each tile's surface above the base.

6. Using a 1/4" straight bit in the router, rout the material from within the borders of each square. Start in the center of each square and work outward.

7. With a 1/2" chisel, square the corners of the routed areas. Then check the fit of both tiles; they should be slightly loose.

8. Cut the board into two pieces down the center of the marked kerf line.

9. Using the 3/8" cove bit in the router, make a test pass along a 1/2"-thick scrap of wood to establish the best bit depth for the decorative edge cuts. Then temporarily insert the tiles, secure the bases, and rout all four edges of each pad.

10. Remove the tiles. Sand each base lightly, place masking tape over the routed areas, and finish the exposed wood (including the bottom surfaces) with three coats of spray lacquer.

11. After removing the tape, spread the tile adhesive evenly over the routed surfaces with a narrow putty knife. Coat the back side of each tile with adhesive, and set the tiles firmly in place.

12. To finish the grout line between the tile and the wood, wipe off the excess adhesive immediately with a damp cloth. Allow the adhesive to dry thoroughly before using your trivets.

Pet Cuisine Tray

Well, all right—Dog Food Bowl-Holder. But whatever you call it (and your dog won't care), you'll appreciate what this simple tray does for the pet whose table manners are less than the best. The lip around its edges will catch every stray crumb and splash. When you're ready to clean the bowls, just lift up the tray.

Materials List

White pine is recommended for this project.

(1)   3/4" x 9-1/4" x 18"   Tray
(2)   3/4" x 1-11/16" x 18"   Sides
(2)   3/4" x 1-11/16" x 10-3/4" Ends

Suggested Tools

Router
45° 7/16" chamfer bit
3/8" drill
3/8" drill bit
Jigsaw
Try square
Compass
36" straightedge
Half-round bastard file
Nail set

Hardware & Supplies

Waterproof wood glue
16-gauge x 1-1/4" brads
Pet bowls (7" base)
Spray polyurethane

Construction Procedure

1. Locate the center of the 9-1/4" x 18" base at 4-5/8", and mark a center line down the length of the board (see Tray Layout).

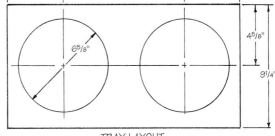

TRAY LAYOUT

2. Measure 4-1/4" from each end, and mark on the center line.

3. With a compass, make one 6-5/8"-diameter circle at each marked point.

4. Drill a 3/8" hole at the inner edge of each circle, and use the jigsaw to cut the circles out.

5. Smooth the circular cuts with a half-round bastard file.

6. Using a chamfer bit in the router, rout both sides of the circles. Sand the base smooth.

7. Strike a line 3/4" from one edge of the side and end pieces.

8. Glue and tack the long side pieces to the edge of the base so that the marked lines are flush with its surface. Repeat the process with the shorter end pieces. Secure each corner with two brads spaced 1" apart.

9. Use a chamfer bit in the router to rout all the frame's outer edges.

10. Sand the project lightly, and finish with several coats of spray polyurethane.

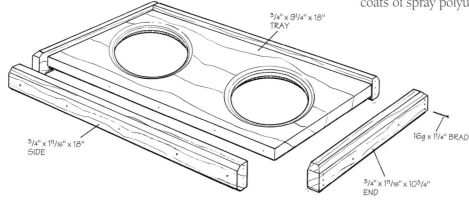

3/4" x 9¼" x 18"
TRAY

3/4" x 1¹¹⁄₁₆" x 18"
SIDE

16g x 1¼" BRAD

3/4" x 1¹¹⁄₁₆" x 10¾"
END

A Tree for Mugs

As well as being attractive, this standing rack is a real space-saver and a definite improvement on cupboards stuffed with stacked mugs. You can use it to suspend a matching set of mugs, or for a bit of color, let each person in the household choose a favorite mug for display.

Materials List

Walnut and white or red oak are recommended for this project.

(1)	1-3/8" x 1-3/8" x 14-1/4"	Walnut post
(1)	3/4" x 7" x 7"	Oak base plate
(6)	3"	Shaker pegs

Suggested Tools

Jigsaw
3/8" drill
1/2" drill bit
No. 8 pilot bit and countersink
Router
1/4" straight bit
3/8" cove bit
1/2" chisel
Hammer
12" straightedge
No. 2 Phillips screwdriver

Hardware & Supplies

Yellow wood glue
No. 8 x 1" flathead wood screw
Spray lacquer

Construction Procedure

1. On the 7" x 7" base plate, locate the center by striking lines diagonally from each top corner to the opposing bottom corner. Strike lines down and across the board through this center point.

2. To locate the post socket, measure and mark lines 11/16" to all four sides of the center mark.

3. To round the base plate's corners, measure 2" in from each of its corners, and mark a point on the diagonal line. With a compass, strike a 2" radius at each corner, using the marks as pivot points.

4. Use a straight bit in the router to make a 3/8"-deep socket in the center of the 1-3/8" square. Clean the corners with a chisel.

5. Cut the marked outline of the base plate with a jigsaw; then sand it smooth.

6. Use a 3/8" cove bit in the router to rout the upper edges of the base plate.

COVE EDGE

14¼"

12"

8½"

5"

½"

POST DETAIL

½" HOLES
½" DEEP

1⅜" x 1⅜" x 14¼"
POST

3" SHAKER PEG

3/8" x 1⅜" x 1⅜"
SOCKET

3/4" x 7" x 7"
BASE PLATE

No. 8 x 1" COUNTERSUNK
SCREW

7. To locate the base end of the post, measure 1/2" from one end of the 14-1/4" post, and mark on all four sides (see Post Detail).

8. Rout a cove edge along each corner of the post's full length, except for the 1/2" base end.

9. On two opposing sides of the post, measure and mark points 5" and 12" up from the base. Then, on the other two sides, measure up 8-1/2" and mark. Strike center lines through each mark.

10. Drill 1/2" holes at each point, each to a depth of 1/2".

11. Sand all the pieces. Then glue the six Shaker pegs into the sockets.

12. Mount the post to the base using glue and a No. 8 x 1" flathead wood screw. Use a No. 8 pilot bit to make the hole, and set the stop collar at 1".

13. Finish the project with several coats of spray lacquer.

Mug Rack

Based on a classic Shaker design, this handy rack is dedicated to those melancholy morning risers who wish that their favorite coffee mugs would stay in one place. If you're tired of starting your day by clawing through the cupboard for your roaming cup, you'll find that this rack is a sure-fire way to keep your mug visible (and waking up worthwhile).

Materials List

Birch is recommended for this project.

(1)	3/4" x 5-7/8" x 21"	Back
(4)	3/8" x 2-1/4"	Shaker pegs

Suggested Tools

Jigsaw
3/8" drill
Compass
36" straightedge
No. 8 pilot bit and counterbore with stop collar
Router
3/8" cove bit
3/8" spade bit

Hardware & Supplies

Yellow wood glue
Spray lacquer

Construction Procedure

1. Measure and mark a line along the length of the 5-7/8" x 21" back piece, 1" in from either edge (see Back Detail).

2. Measure and mark points on this line, 3-3/4" in from each end. Then measure in 8-1/4" from each end, and make a second set of marks on the line.

3. At these four points, use the 3/8" spade bit to drill 3/8"-deep holes in the board.

4. Measure and mark the board's center (at 2-15/16") with a line.

5. Measure in 3" from each end of the board, and mark at this line. Strike a 3" radius at each end of the board, using these two marks as the pivot points for your compass.

6. With a jigsaw, cut each radius as marked.

7. Using the 3/8" cove bit in the router, rout all the edges of the board's front face.

8. With the No. 8 pilot bit, countersink two mounting holes at the 1" line, centering them 16" apart.

9. Fasten the pegs to the back piece with yellow wood glue.

10. Sand the project lightly, and finish with several coats of spray lacquer.

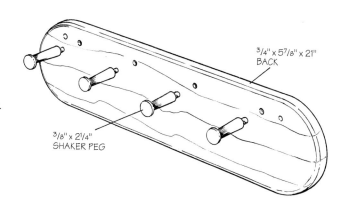

3/4" x 5 7/8" x 21"
BACK

3/8" x 2 1/4"
SHAKER PEG

Snack Rack

Children's afternoon snacks can easily turn into junk-food extravaganzas. Keep your kids healthy (and happy) by limiting their between-meal treats to the fresh fruit, whole-grain chips, and nuts that you leave in this rack each day. Of course, if your family has its eating habits under control already, you can use this handy project to keep track of the dog's leash, the week's mail, or the month's bills instead!

Materials List

Birch is recommended for this project.

(1)	3/4" x 6" x 13"	Sides
(1)	3/4" x 7-5/8" x 14"	Back
(10)	1/2" x 3/4" x 14"	Slats

Suggested Tools

3/8" drill
1-1/4" spade bit
No. 6 pilot bit and countersink with stop collar
No. 8 pilot bit and countersink with stop collar
Router
3/8" roundover bit
Jigsaw
12" straightedge
Compass
No. 2 Phillips screwdriver

Hardware & Supplies

No. 8 x 1" flathead wood screws
No. 6 x 3/4" flathead brass wood screws
Spray lacquer

Construction Procedure

1. Both of the rack's sides are marked and cut from the 6" x 13" board. Begin by marking two 6" radii on its face, using the two upper corners as pivot points for your compass.

2. Next, measure 2" down and 2" in from these same two corners, and mark lines within each quadrant. Drill a 1-1/4" hole with a spade bit at each set of intersecting points (see Slat Detail).

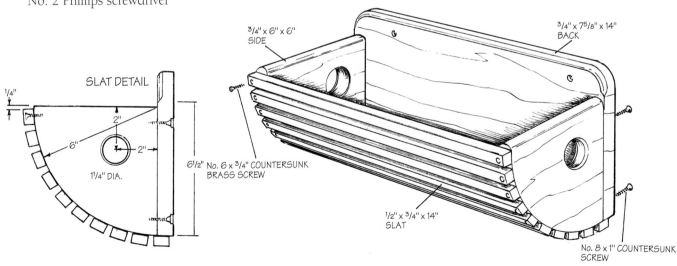

SLAT DETAIL
1/4"
2"
6"
2"
1 1/4" DIA.
6 1/2"   No. 6 x 3/4" COUNTERSUNK BRASS SCREW
3/4" x 6" x 6" SIDE
3/4" x 7 5/8" x 14" BACK
1/2" x 3/4" x 14" SLAT
No. 8 x 1" COUNTERSUNK SCREW

3. Use a 3/8" roundover bit to round the edges of both holes on both faces of the board. Then round both faces of the 13" edge from which the two radii were struck.

4. Cut along the radius lines with a jigsaw, and sand the two side pieces smooth.

5. To mark the rounded upper corners of the 7-5/8" x 14" back piece, first measure 1" in from each of its ends and 1" down from one edge, marking lines at both corners.

6. Then strike a 1" radius from each of these points across the upper corners. Use a jigsaw to cut along the radius lines, and sand the corners smooth.

7. Measure 6-1/2" up from the square-cornered edge, and mark on both ends of the board (see Slat Detail). Use the 3/8" roundover bit to round the upper edge and the two rounded corners on the board's face, routing only as far as the 6-1/2" marks. Sand the edges smooth.

8. Position the sides flush with the back's ends, and use the No. 8 pilot bit to drill holes 4-1/2" apart, through the back and into the side's edges. Set the stop collar at 1-1/4". Use No. 8 x 1" flathead screws as fasteners.

9. On the face side of each of the 3/4" x 14" slats, round the end corners slightly.

10. Measure down 1/4" from the top edge of each side piece, and use this point to position the first slat's upper edge (see Slat Detail). The 3/4" face of the slat should be the one showing. Fasten the slat by drilling a hole with the No. 6 pilot bit through each slat end and into the sides' edges. Set the stop collar at 7/8", and use No. 6 x 3/4" flathead brass screws as fasteners.

11. Fasten the remaining slats to the sides, using a pencil as a spacer to gauge the distance between each slat.

12. Finish the project with several coats of spray lacquer.

Kitchen Towel Rack

Have you ever wondered why your kitchen towels sometimes smell musty even when they're clean? That unwelcome odor may be a result of your tossing damp towels over open cupboard doors or squeezing them through cabinet handles, where they never have a chance to dry out properly. This dowel rack, which allows fresh air to circulate freely, will let your towels dry quickly and will keep them fresh far longer.

Materials List

Black walnut is recommended for this project.

(1)	3/4" x 4" x 16"	Back
(1)	1-1/4" x 20"	Birch dowel bar
(2)	3/4" x 2-1/2"	Birch dowel supports

Suggested Tools

Try square
36" straightedge
Compass
C-clamps
Jigsaw
3/8" drill
3/4" spade bit
No. 8 pilot bit and counterbore with stop collar
No. 2 Phillips screwdriver

Hardware & Supplies

Yellow wood glue
No. 8 x 1-1/4" flathead wood screws
3/8" dowel plugs
Spray lacquer

Construction Procedure

1. Strike a center line along the face of the 4" x 16" back piece, and mark the center of the piece's length at this line (see Back Detail).

2. Measure 3-1/2" in from each end of the board, and mark at the line. Then, using these two points as pivots for your compass, strike a 3-1/2" radius at each end of the board.

3. With a jigsaw, cut along the curved lines.

4. Measure 1-5/8" to each side of the back piece's marked center, and mark on the center line.

5. Using the 3/4" spade bit, drill a hole to a depth of 3/8" at these two points. Then replace the spade bit with the No. 8 pilot bit; using the pilot holes already established, drill through the sockets just enough to penetrate the back side of the board.

6. Measure and mark the center of the 20" dowel bar. Then mark 1-5/8" to each side of this center.

7. Clamp the bar between two 1-1/4"-thick boards on a bench top. Use the try square to find the center of the bar's width, and mark it at each of the 1-5/8" points.

8. With the spade bit, drill 3/4" holes to a depth of 5/8" at these two points on the dowel bar. Then use the pilot bit as before to penetrate the opposite face of the bar.

9. Glue the 3/4" x 2-1/2" dowel supports into the 4" x 16" back piece and into the 1-1/4" x 20" dowel bar.

10. With the No. 8 pilot bit and counterbore (and a stop collar set at 1-1/2"), drill four holes, two through

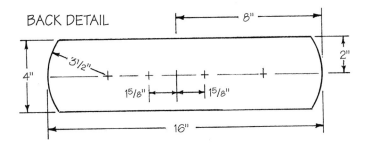

BACK DETAIL

114

the 1-1/4" dowel and into the dowel supports, and two through the back and into the other ends of the dowel supports. Use the visible drill holes that you created in Steps 5 and 8 as guides.

11. Secure the dowel supports to the 1-1/4" dowel bar and to the back piece with four No. 8 x 1-1/4" flat-head wood screws.

12. Plug the recessed screw holes in the dowel bar and back with 3/8" dowel plugs, and then sand them flush.

13. Use the No. 8 pilot bit and counterbore to drill two mounting holes through the back, centered at a distance to suit your installation needs.

14. After sanding the project lightly, apply several coats of spray lacquer.

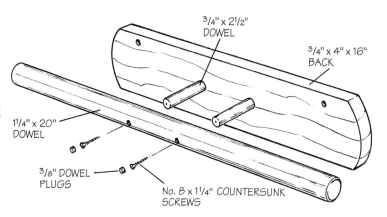

Towel Bar

For most kitchens, a small rack provides plenty of space for a kitchen towel or two, but for larger households, this hefty two-dowel rack may be more appropriate. The simple design is sturdy and stylish; contrasting woods provide an eye-catching backdrop for even the plainest of towels. Don't forget to mount this project within easy reach of the sink.

Materials List

Black walnut is recommended for this project.

(1)	3/4" x 4-1/2" x 32-1/2"	Back and arms
(2)	3/4" x 36"	Dowel bars

Suggested Tools

Jigsaw
Crosscut handsaw
Try square
36" straightedge
3/8" drill
3/4" spade bit
No. 8 pilot bit and counterbore with stop collar
No. 2 Phillips screwdriver

Hardware & Supplies

Yellow wood glue
No. 8 x 1" flathead wood screws
Spray lacquer

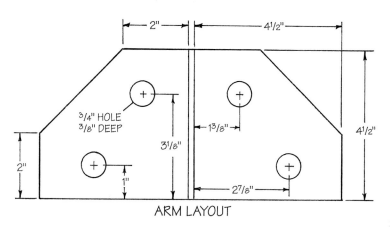

ARM LAYOUT

Construction Procedure

1. Cut a 23" back piece from the 4-1/2" board.

2. On the piece remaining, measure and mark two 4-1/2"-square arm pieces by marking lines across the board, 4-1/2" in from each end.

3. To establish the angled cutting line on the arms, measure and mark two points on each square, one 2" up from one lower corner and the other 2" in from the diagonal upper corner (see Arm Layout). Mark and then draw a diagonal line between the two marks on each piece.

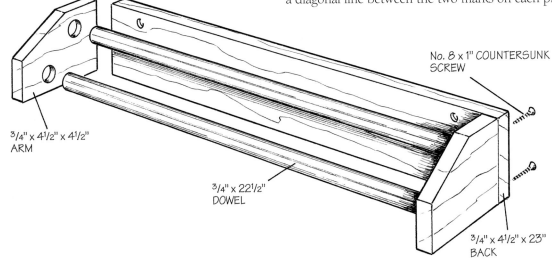

3/4" x 4-1/2" x 4-1/2"
ARM

3/4" x 22-1/2"
DOWEL

No. 8 x 1" COUNTERSUNK
SCREW

3/4" x 4-1/2" x 23"
BACK

4. With a handsaw, cut each 4-1/2" piece to length, and then use a jigsaw to cut the diagonals. Sand both arms smooth.

5. Find the bottom 4-1/2" edge on each piece; the wood grain should run parallel to it. From that edge, measure up 1" and mark a line; then measure up 3-1/8" and mark a line.

6. From the remaining long edge, measure in 1-3/8" and mark a point to intersect with the 3-1/8" line; also measure in 2-7/8" and mark a point to intersect with the 1" line.

7. Using the 3/4" spade bit, drill two 3/8"-deep holes into each arm at the points marked. Do not let the drill point penetrate the opposite side of the arm.

8. Cut each of the two 3/4" dowels to 22-1/2" in length. Sand all the pieces.

9. Position the arms at each end of the back piece, and using the No. 8 pilot bit and counterbore, drill holes 3-1/4" apart into the back of the board so that they penetrate the ends of the arms. Set the stop collar at 1-1/4".

10. Fasten one arm with glue and No. 8 x 1" flat-head wood screws. Slip the dowels into their sockets, and then fasten the second arm in the same manner.

11. Mark a line 3/4" from the back's top edge. Center a pair of marks on each line, 16" apart. With the No. 8 pilot bit, drill and countersink two mounting holes.

12. Sand all edges and faces of the project, and apply three coats of spray lacquer to finish the wood.

Dowel Shelf

Even though it won't hold crystal stemware or the family china, this dowel shelf offers two advantages that a solid shelf can't. It adds a bit of airiness to an otherwise dark or crowded kitchen, and its dowel surface can be used as a towel rack, too. Whether you stock the shelf with coffee, decorate it with a favorite houseplant, or drape a pretty towel around one dowel, you'll find that this easy-to-build project is as attractive as it is useful.

Materials List

White or red oak is recommended for this project.

(2)	3/4" x 4-3/4" x 6-1/2"	Supports
(1)	3/4" x 2-1/2" x 16"	Brackets
(4)	3/4" x 36"	Birch dowels

Suggested Tools

Router
3/4" straight bit
3/8" drill
3/4" spade bit
Jigsaw
36" straightedge
No. 8 pilot bit and countersink with stop collar
No. 2 Phillips screwdriver
Compass
Tack hammer

Hardware & Supplies

No. 8 x 1" flathead wood screws
16-gauge x 1-1/4" brads
Spray lacquer

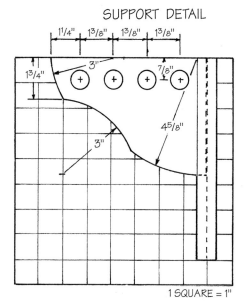

SUPPORT DETAIL

1 SQUARE = 1"

Construction Procedure

1. Lay out each 4-3/4" x 6-1/2" support piece by referring to the Support Detail illustration and to the instructions that follow. With one long edge of each support to the bottom, measure over 1/2" from the lower left end of each, and strike a 3" radius from this point. Then, at the top left end of the support, measure over 3" and strike a 3" radius at this point to intersect with the first arc. Finally, measure 3" further from the second point, and strike a 4-5/8" radius that intersects with the first arc.

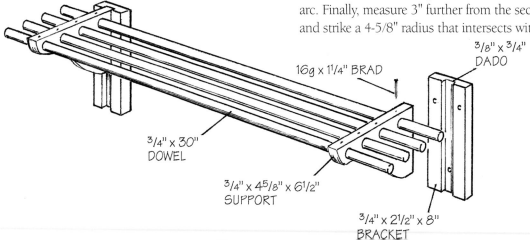

3/4" x 30"
DOWEL

16g x 1¹/₄" BRAD

3/8" x 3/4"
DADO

3/4" x 4⁵/₈" x 6¹/₂"
SUPPORT

3/4" x 2¹/₂" x 8"
BRACKET

2. Measure down 7/8" from the top edge of each piece (the one opposite to the arcs), and strike a straight line parallel to this edge.

3. Starting from the point at which the second arc meets the top edge, mark each piece along the line at the following points: 1-1/4", 1-3/8", 1-3/8", and 1-3/8".

4. With a 3/4" spade bit, drill holes at the marked centers.

5. Use a jigsaw to cut each support to shape.

6. Use a router and a straight bit to rout a 3/4"-wide, 3/8"-deep slot down the center of the 16" bracket piece.

7. Cut the bracket piece into two 8" lengths.

8. Cut each of the four 3/4" dowels to 30" in length.

9. Sand all the wooden parts.

10. Place the supports into the brackets' slots, flush with the tops of the brackets. Fasten them in place with No. 8 x 1" flathead wood screws drilled in from the back. Use a No. 8 pilot bit, and set the stop collar at 1-1/4". Countersunk mounting holes can be drilled at this time, too. The upper pair should be set 1-1/2" from the top edge, and the lower one centered in the brackets' slots, 2" from the bottom edge.

11. Slip the dowels through the supports' holes so that 3" protrudes from each dowel end. Secure each dowel with 16-gauge brads nailed through the supports' top edges.

12. Sand and finish the project with several coats of spray polyurethane.

Narrow Shelf

Like its wider counterpart on page 122, this project was designed to save otherwise wasted wall space. The narrow shelf won't hold quite as much, but its size makes it perfect for small kitchens. Whether you use this project to store knickknacks or to display your heirloom china, you'll find that it's practical, attractive, and easy to make.

Materials List

White pine and white or red oak are recommended for this project.

(1)   3/4" x 3" x 42"   Frame
(1)   3/4" x 4-7/8" x 30-7/8"   Pine shelf

Suggested Tools

Router
3/8" roundover bit
1/2" straight bit
3/8" drill
No. 8 pilot bit and countersink with stop collar
Circular saw
36" straightedge
No. 2 Phillips screwdriver

Hardware & Supplies

Yellow wood glue
No. 8 x 1" flathead wood screws
3/8" dowel plugs
Spray polyurethane

Construction Procedure

1. Using a straight bit in the router, dado a 3/4"-wide, 3/8"-deep slot in the 42" frame piece, centering it 1-1/2" from the edge (see Dado Detail).

2. Cut the frame piece into one 30-1/8" length and two 5-1/4" lengths.

3. Fasten the shorter side pieces to the ends of the long piece with No. 8 x 1" flathead screws, making sure that the dado slots are aligned with each other. Set the stop collar on the No. 8 pilot bit at 1-1/4".

4. Use the roundover bit in the router to dress both edges of one long side of the shelf.

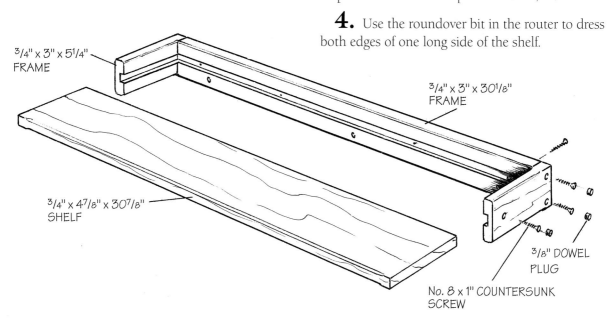

3/4" x 3" x 5 1/4"
FRAME

3/4" x 3" x 30 1/8"
FRAME

3/4" x 4 7/8" x 30 7/8"
SHELF

3/8" DOWEL PLUG

No. 8 x 1" COUNTERSUNK SCREW

5. Slide the pine shelf into the dadoes, with its routed edge facing outward. If the fit is tight, sand the edges of the shelf.

6. Secure the shelf to the frame with countersunk No. 8 x 1" flathead screws, placing one screw through each side piece and three through the back, spaced 12" apart. Set the pilot bit stop collar at 1-1/8".

7. Use the roundover bit in the router to round all the frame's edges.

8. Plug all the counterbored screw holes with 3/8" dowel plugs, glued in place. Sand the plugs flush with the surface of the wood.

9. Sand the entire project lightly.

10. Finish the completed shelf with several coats of spray polyurethane.

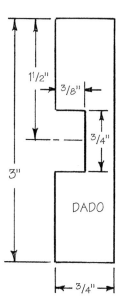

DADO DETAIL

Wide Shelf

An extra shelf in the kitchen can sometimes mean the difference between gratifying order and culinary chaos. This one will fit almost anywhere: under a cupboard, over a range, or right by the back door. Stock it with frequently used kitchenware—those items you can never find when they're hidden in drawers—or use its broad surface to display your kitchen treasures.

Materials List

White pine and cherry are recommended for this project.

(1) 3/4" x 3" x 60"   Cherry frame
(1) 3/4" x 11-3/8" x 29-5/8" Pine shelf

Suggested Tools

Router
1/2" straight bit
5/32" ogee bit
Backsaw and miter box
Circular saw
3/8" drill bit
No. 8 pilot bit and countersink with stop collar
Tack hammer
36" straightedge
No. 2 Phillips screwdriver

Hardware & Supplies

Yellow wood glue
No. 8 x 1-1/4" flathead wood screws
16-gauge x 3/4" brads
3/8" dowel plugs
8" shelf brackets
Spray polyurethane

Construction Procedure

1. Use a straight bit in the router to cut a 3/4"-wide, 3/8"-deep dado in the 60" frame piece. To mark the borders of the dado slot, strike a full-length line 1-1/4" from one edge and another line 3/4" from the first (see Dado Detail).

2. To miter the corners of the frame, first cut a 45°

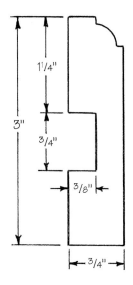

DADO DETAIL

angle on one end of the piece, making sure that the dado slot will run along the shorter face of the frame. On the side opposite to the dado, measure over 30-3/8" from the angled end, and cut a second 45° angle in the opposite direction.

3. On the remaining piece, cut a 45° angle on one end so that the dado slot in it will align with the matching end of the long frame piece. Measure 11-3/4" from the mitered end (on the side without the dado), and make a square cut.

4. Match the dado of the piece remaining to the other mitered end of the long frame piece. Cut a 45° angle in that end of the final frame piece, measure 11-3/4" from the mitered end, and make another square cut.

5. Trim the shelf board to a length of 29-5/8".

6. Sand the faces of all the wooden pieces.

7. Apply glue to the mitered corners of the frame pieces, checking to be sure that the dadoes are aligned. Tack the frame together with brads so that the frame won't shift as you drill screw holes in it. (Don't place brads where they're likely to interfere with the screws that you'll be inserting next.)

8. Set the No. 8 pilot bit's stop collar at 1-1/2", and space two screw holes, 1-3/4" apart, through the short sides of the frame. Fasten the glued corners permanently with No. 8 x 1-1/4" flathead screws.

9. Slide the shelf board into the dadoes. Sand the edges if necessary to make the board fit.

10. Fasten the shelf to the frame using No. 8 x 1-1/4" flathead screws placed through the side frame pieces. Set the pilot bit's stop collar at 1-3/8".

11. Using an ogee bit in the router, rout the upper face edge of the frame all around.

12. Plug all the screw holes with 3/8" dowel plugs, glued in place. Sand them flush with the surface of the wood.

13. Sand the project lightly, and finish it with several coats of spray polyurethane.

14. Fasten the 8" shelf brackets to the bottom and flush with the back, using the hardware provided.

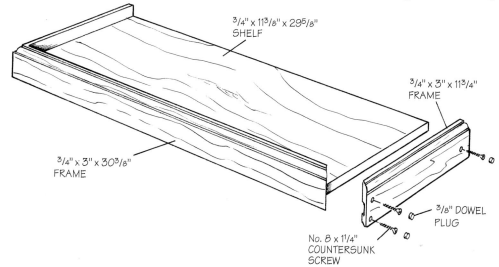

3/4" x 11³/₈" x 29⁵/₈"
SHELF

3/4" x 3" x 11³/₄"
FRAME

3/4" x 3" x 30³/₈"
FRAME

3/8" DOWEL
PLUG

No. 8 x 1¹/₄"
COUNTERSUNK
SCREW

Stacking Onion Bins

Neither onions nor potatoes fare well in the refrigerator, but they don't need a root cellar to be happy. These stacking bins, placed in a cool kitchen corner, will do just as well. The bins' pegboard bottoms permit air to circulate freely, their walls will protect the contents from damaging sunlight, and their front openings are just large enough to let you empty or refill each bin without having to disassemble the stack.

Materials List

The listed materials will make one bin. White pine is suggested for this project.

(2)	3/4" x 8" x 17-1/2"	Sides
(2)	3/4" x 7-1/4" x 10-1/16"	Front and rear panels
(1)	1/4" x 10-9/16" x 16-1/2"	Pegboard

Suggested Tools

3/8" drill
No. 8 pilot bit and countersink with stop collar
Router
1/2" straight bit
Jigsaw
Compass
36" straightedge
No. 2 Phillips screwdriver

Hardware & Supplies

No. 8 x 1" flathead wood screws
Food-grade bowl finish

Construction Procedure

1. On each 8" x 17-1/2" side piece, use the straight bit to cut a dado 3/8" wide and 7/16" deep, the length of one long edge. Repeat this procedure on the opposite edge of each piece's other face.

2. To locate 1/4" dadoes for the pegboard, on one dadoed face of each side piece, measure 3/8" up from the top of the existing dado, and strike a line lengthwise along the side's face (see Side Detail). Measure up 1/4" from that line, and strike a second line. Then dado a 1/4" x 1/4" channel between the marked lines on both boards.

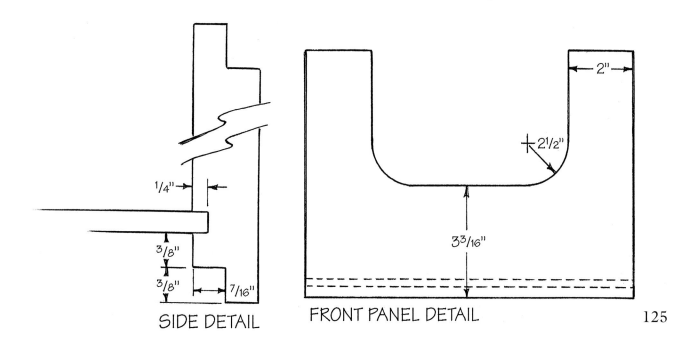

SIDE DETAIL

FRONT PANEL DETAIL

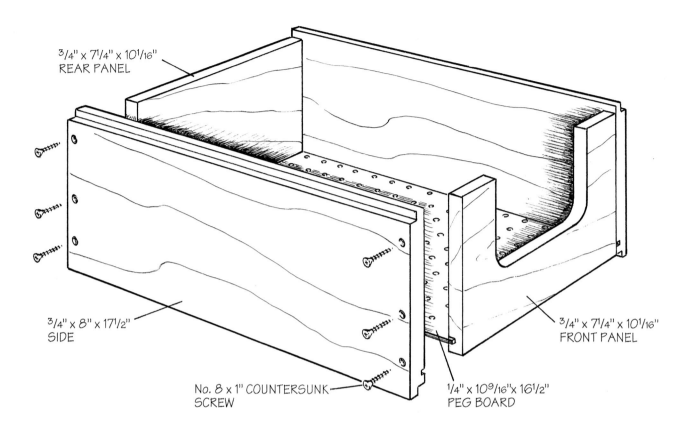

3/4" x 7-1/4" x 10-1/16"
REAR PANEL

3/4" x 8" x 17-1/2"
SIDE

No. 8 x 1" COUNTERSUNK
SCREW

1/4" x 10-9/16" x 16-1/2"
PEG BOARD

3/4" x 7-1/4" x 10-1/16"
FRONT PANEL

3. To create a matching pegboard dado in the 7-1/4" x 10-1/16" front and rear panels, measure and mark lines 3/8" and 5/8" up from their bottom edges, and repeat the dadoing process to make 1/4"-deep dadoes in each piece.

4. Locate the center of the length of one 7-1/4" x 10-1/16" panel, and strike a line across the width of the board. Measure 3-3/16" from the dadoed edge, and strike a lengthwise line (see Front Panel Detail). From each top corner, measure 2" in, along the panel's top edge, and strike a line down to the 3-3/16" line.

5. From each side of the corners created by the 3-3/16" line and the 2" lines, measure 2-1/2" in, and mark. From the intersection of these 2-1/2" marks, strike a 2-1/2" radius at each inside corner.

6. Use a jigsaw to cut the marked opening from the board. This piece will be the front panel. Sand its edges and faces.

7. Fasten the sides to the rear panel with No. 8 x 1" flathead screws, placed 2-3/4" apart. Use a No. 8 pilot bit to drill the holes, and set the stop collar at 1-1/4". The 1/4" dado channels should be aligned, and the lower edge of the rear panel should be flush with the top of the adjoining 3/8" dadoes.

8. Slide the pegboard into the dadoes of the three-sided bin. Position and mount the front panel using the same method as before. Sand the wood lightly.

9. Finish the bin with a food-grade bowl finish. (For greater durability, you can use spray polyurethane instead.) The bin is designed to stack upon others, so you can make matching sets if you wish.

10. You can easily make a cover for the bin by routing a 3/8" x 3/8" dado down the sides of a pine board measuring 11-9/16" x 17-1/2". Start the dadoes 3/8" from each long edge.

Note Board

Are these stories familiar? You write a grocery list on a paper napkin—and ten minutes later, throw the napkin away. Your cat achieves his life's goal—by rolling the last kitchen pencil under the refrigerator. You leave an urgent message on the counter, and it drifts gently behind the cupboard as soon as you leave the house. Put an end to these kitchen communications nightmares with a note board. This one boasts a pencil-pocket, a surface you can write on, and a shelf to hold the note-pad, too.

Materials List

Walnut is recommended for this project.

(2)	3/4" x 1-3/4" x 20-1/8"	Frame sides
(1)	3/4" x 1-3/4" x 13-1/2"	Upper frame
(1)	3/4" x 4-1/4" x 13-1/2"	Lower frame
(1)	3/4" x 3-1/2" x 13-1/2"	Tray front
(2)	3/4" x 3-1/2" x 3-1/4"	Tray sides
(1)	3/4" x 1-3/4" x 12"	Pencil holder
(1)	1/4" x 14-7/16" x 19-9/16"	Tile board back

Suggested Tools

3/8" drill
3/8" drill bit
No. 8 pilot bit and countersink with stop collar
Router
3/8" roundover bit
1/2" straight bit
36" straightedge
No. 2 Phillips screwdriver
Backsaw
Miter box
Smooth file
Tack hammer

Hardware & Supplies

No. 8 x 1" flathead wood screws
18-gauge x 3/4" brads
3/8" dowel plugs
3-1/2" decorative handles (2)
Spray lacquer

Construction Procedure

1. Fasten the 1-3/4" x 13-1/2" upper frame between the two 1-3/4" x 20-1/8" frame sides, using No. 8 x 1" flathead wood screws. Use a No. 8 pilot bit to drill holes 7/8" apart, through the frame sides' faces and into the upper frame's ends. Set the stop collar at 1-1/4".

2. Fasten the 4-1/4" x 13-1/2" lower frame to the edge of the 3-1/2" x 13-1/2" tray front with No. 8 x 1" flathead screws placed 5-1/2" apart. Use the same method as in Step 1.

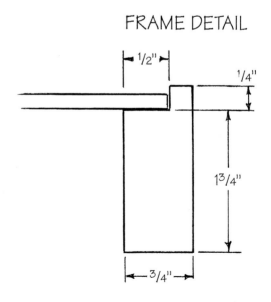

FRAME DETAIL

3. Position the two 3-1/2" x 3-1/4" tray sides on top of the lower frame, flush with the tray front's edges. Fasten the tray sides in place using two No. 8 x 1" flat-head screws at each end of the lower frame, spaced 1-1/2" apart, and inserted through the bottom of the lower frame. (Note that these screws are not shown in the illustration.) Set the stop collar at 1-1/4".

4. Drill one hole in each upper corner of the tray front, and install No. 8 x 1" flathead screws into the tray side's edges.

5. Measure and mark 1-3/4" in from the back end of each tray side. Then use a 3/8" roundover bit to round the inside upper edges of the assembled box. Round the outside upper and lower edges to the lines just marked.

6. On the 20-1/8" frame sides, measure up 4-3/4" from the bottom end, and mark on the inside. Use a 3/8" roundover bit to round the inside edge of the frame to those points, leaving the ends square. Rout both outside edges of the frame and the ends.

7. Mount the tray assembly inside the frame, flush with the bottom and rear edges. To attach the tray assembly, use two No. 8 x 1" screws on each side of the frame, spaced 3-1/2" apart. Set the stop collar at 1-1/4".

8. Round both sides of one edge of the 1-3/4" x 12" strip, using the 3/8" roundover bit. Cut a 4-1/4" length from the piece, and make holes for pencils by drilling two 3/8"-wide, 2-1/2"-deep holes in one end. (Keep in mind that the holder's rounded edge is its front edge.)

9. Mount the pencil holder to the side of the tray, against the frame side's edge and flush with its bottom end. Attach it with two No. 8 x 1" flathead screws spaced 3-1/2" apart. Set the pilot bit's stop collar at 1-1/4".

10. Turn the assembled frame so that its back is facing up. With a 1/2" straight bit, rout a 1/2"-wide, 1/4"-deep dado around the inside edge of the frame.

11. With a smooth-cut file, round the corners of the tile board, and check its fit within the frame's dado.

12. Plug all the screw holes with 3/8" dowel plugs glued in place. Sand the plugs flush with the wood's surface.

13. Drill mounting holes for the handles in the upper and lower frame pieces. Use the No. 8 pilot bit to counterbore the screw openings from the inside.

14. Sand the frame and tray, and finish the assembly with several coats of spray lacquer.

15. Mount the handles with the hardware provided.

16. Use 3/4" brads to fasten the tile board (with its white face to the front) within the frame's dado channel.

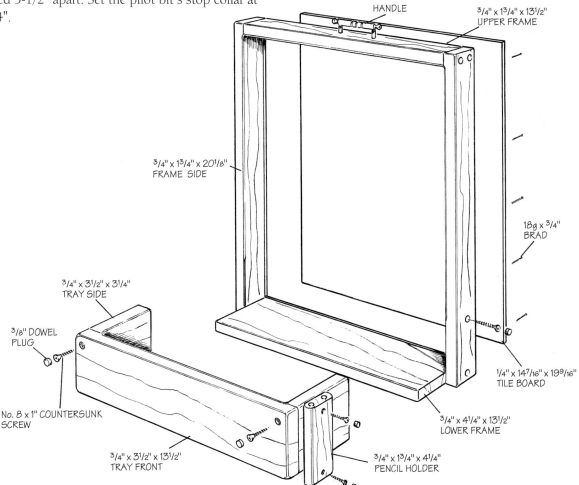

HANDLE

3/4" x 1³/4" x 13¹/2"
UPPER FRAME

3/4" x 1³/4" x 20¹/8"
FRAME SIDE

18g x ³/4"
BRAD

3/4" x 3¹/2" x 3¹/4"
TRAY SIDE

3/8" DOWEL
PLUG

1/4" x 14⁷/16" x 19⁹/16"
TILE BOARD

No. 8 x 1" COUNTERSUNK
SCREW

3/4" x 4¹/4" x 13¹/2"
LOWER FRAME

3/4" x 3¹/2" x 13¹/2"
TRAY FRONT

3/4" x 1³/4" x 4¹/4"
PENCIL HOLDER

Cork Board

Start hoarding used wine corks today; you'll need quite a few of them for this note board! And while you're waiting for your collection to grow, build the board's frame. The corks (sliced in half for easy gluing) will hold grocery lists, reminders, postcards, telephone massages, and more. When they're so full of holes that they won't hold your push pins any more, just replace them with new ones.

Materials List

Cypress is recommended for this project.

(2)	3/4" x 1-7/8" x 26"	Side frames
(2)	3/4" x 1-7/8" x 21"	Upper and lower frames
(1)	1/4" x 14-3/8" x 19-1/8"	Plywood tile board
(1)	3/4" x 1-7/8" x 16-3/4"	Ledge
(1)	1/4" x 3/4" x 16"	Trim board

Suggested Tools

3/8" drill
1/16" drill bit
No. 8 pilot bit and countersink with stop collar
Router
3/8" roundover bit
36" straightedge
No. 2 Phillips screwdriver
Coping saw
Backsaw
Miter box
Tack hammer

Hardware & Supplies

Yellow wood glue
Spray adhesive
18-gauge x 3/4" brads
16-gauge x 1-1/4" brads
No. 8 x 1" flathead wood screws
Wine bottle corks
Spray lacquer

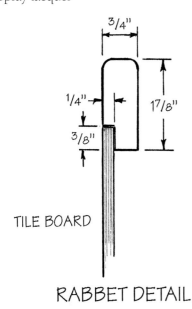

TILE BOARD

RABBET DETAIL

Construction Procedure

1. Using a 3/8" roundover bit, round both sides of one edge of the 21" and 26" frame strips.

2. Switch to the 1/2" straight bit, and cut a 3/8"-wide by 1/4"-deep rabbet along one square edge of all four strips (see Rabbet Detail).

3. With a backsaw and miter box, cut opposing 45° angles at the ends of the 26" strips so that the longest edge of each one is 22" in length. The rabbet must be to the back, on the short edge of these side frame pieces.

4. Cut opposing 45° angles at the ends of the 22" strips so that the longest edges are 17-3/8" in length. Again, the rabbet must be to the back, on the short edge of these upper and lower frame pieces.

5. Assemble the frame by gluing the joining edges and securing them with two 1-1/4" brads at each corner.

6. Place the plywood tile board into the frame (brown face showing), and run a pencil mark all round the board where it meets the inside edges of the frame. Remove the plywood, and strike a line 3/4" above the bottom line just marked.

7. Cut the corks in half lengthwise with a coping saw.

8. Apply the spray adhesive within the marked borders of the tile board's face. (Note that the 3/4" marked strip at the board's bottom should not be sprayed.)

9. In any pattern you choose, lay out the cork sections (flat side down) within the marked boundaries. Refer to the adhesive container to establish how much time you have to complete the work before the glue sets. It may be necessary to complete the gluing in two or more sessions.

10. On the 16-3/4" ledge, measure and mark a line 1-1/2" from each end. Measure and mark a line lengthwise, 1/2" from one edge. Cut out the marked rectangular corners with a coping saw.

11. Use a 3/8" roundover bit in the router to round the ends and front on both faces. Sand the edges.

12. Place the 3/4" x 16" trim board onto the ledge's lower face so that its back edge is flush with the longest edges of the ledge's cut-out rectangles. Glue the pieces together, and fasten them with 3/4" brads.

13. Use the 3/8" roundover bit to rout a shallow, round lower edge on the 3/4" x 16" trim board. Sand well.

14. Fit the plywood tile board into the frame's back, and slip the ledge into place so that the tile board's uncorked area is covered.

15. Mount the tile board to the edges of the frame using 3/4" brads driven from the back side. Fasten the ledge to the frame with No. 8 x 1" flathead screws, one driven through the back of each side frame. Use a No. 8 pilot bit, and set the stop collar at 1-1/4".

16. Drill mounting holes in the upper and lower frame faces, using the No. 8 pilot bit and countersink.

17. Lightly sand the cypress surface, avoiding the cork pieces as you do.

18. Tape newspaper over the cork face, and finish the frame with several coats of spray lacquer.

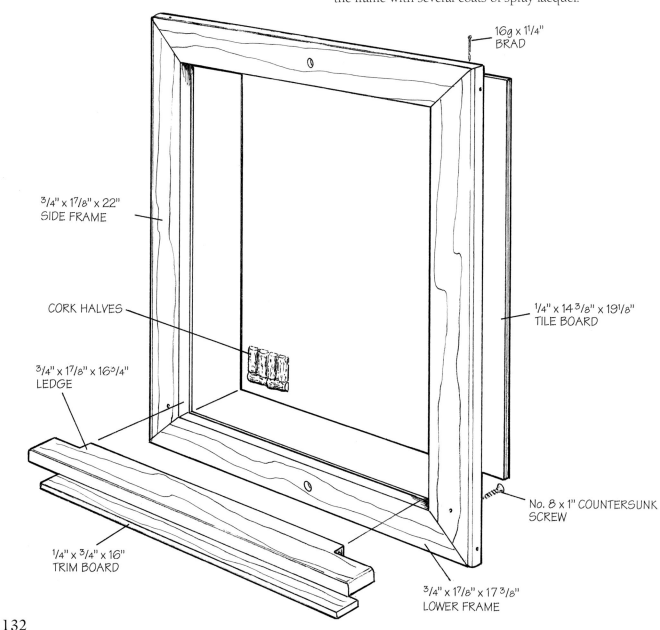

16g x 1 1/4" BRAD

3/4" x 1 7/8" x 22" SIDE FRAME

1/4" x 14 3/8" x 19 1/8" TILE BOARD

CORK HALVES

3/4" x 1 7/8" x 16 3/4" LEDGE

No. 8 x 1" COUNTERSUNK SCREW

1/4" x 3/4" x 16" TRIM BOARD

3/4" x 1 7/8" x 17 3/8" LOWER FRAME

Magazine Rack

More happens in most kitchens than cooking. We amble in for snacks, we make phone calls, and yes, we sometimes read. Unfortunately, we also tend to leave our magazines and open mail behind us, until printed matter begins to claim every counter and table top in sight. This simple rack will rescue precious work space in no time at all. Attach it to any kitchen wall, and watch how quickly it clears up those mountains of paper.

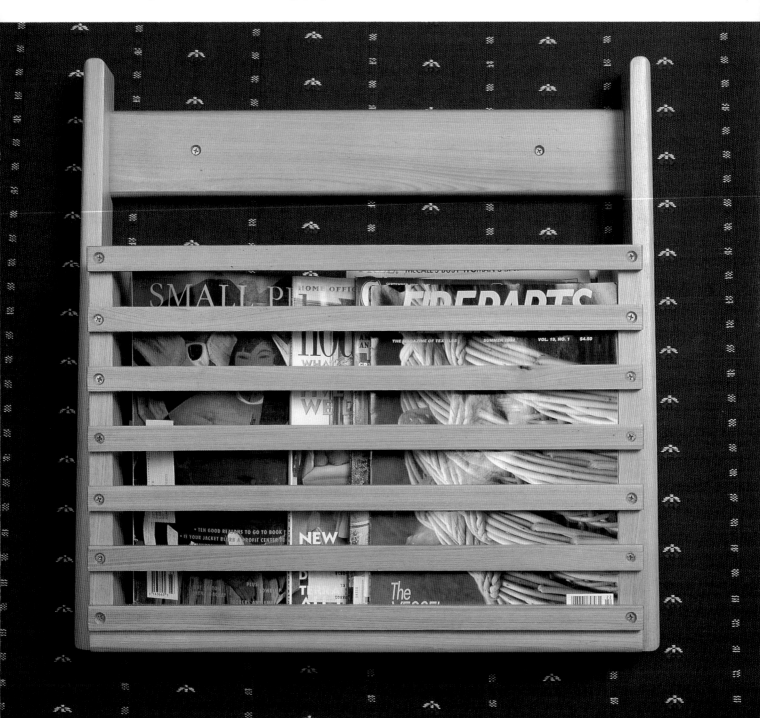

Materials List

Cypress is recommended for this project.

(2)	3/4" x 2" x 19-1/2"	Sides
(2)	3/4" x 3" x 18"	Top slat and bottom shelf
(2)	3/4" x 4" x 12"	Slat supports
(7)	3/8" x 3/4" x 18"	Front slats

Suggested Tools

Table saw
36" straightedge
3/8" drill
No. 6 pilot bit and countersink with stop collar
No. 8 pilot bit and countersink with stop collar
No. 2 Phillips screwdriver
Router
3/8" roundover bit

Hardware & Supplies

No. 6 x 3/4" brass flathead wood screws
No. 8 x 1" flathead wood screws
3/8" dowel plugs
Spray lacquer

Construction Procedure

1. Using the 3/8" roundover bit in the router, round the following edges on each of the two 2" x 19-1/2" sides: the two long edges on one face, the short bottom edge of the same face, and both short top edges.

2. Also round both long edges on one face of one 3" x 18" piece and one long edge of the other 3" x 18" piece.

3. Draw a diagonal across the face of each 4" x 12" piece so that one end of the line is 1/8" from one long edge and the other is 1" from the same edge (see Slat Support Layout). Cut along the line, and discard the smaller portion of each piece. The remaining pieces will be the two slat supports.

4. Use a table saw, with the rip fence set at 3/8", to cut seven 3/8" x 3/4" x 18" slats from a 3/4" board measuring 5" x 18" or wider.

5. Place the ends of the two angle-cut slat supports against the 3" x 18" bottom shelf so that the shelf's one rounded edge leads into the angled edges of the supports. Use the No. 8 pilot bit, with its stop collar set at 1-1/4", to drill screw holes through the shelf and into the supports. Fasten the pieces together with No. 8 x 1" flathead wood screws.

6. Place the side pieces, with their rounded ends up, against the outside of the slat supports so that the bottom and back edges of the sides and supports are even.

7. With the No. 8 pilot bit, drill three holes through each side, spaced about 5" apart and 3/8" from the back edge. Set the stop collar at 1-1/4". Fasten the sides to the supports with No. 8 x 1" flathead wood screws.

8. Position the 3" x 18" top slat between the two sides so that its bottom edge is 2-1/4" from the top of the slat supports and its rounded edges face toward the front. Its back face should be flush with the rear edges of each side piece.

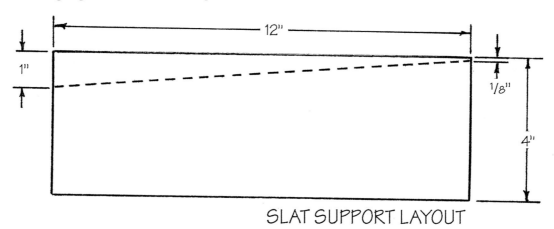

SLAT SUPPORT LAYOUT

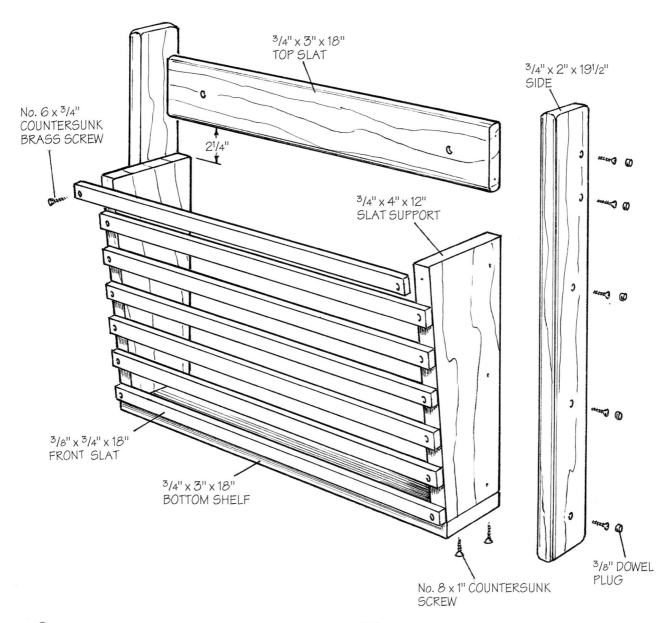

3/4" x 3" x 18"
TOP SLAT

3/4" x 2" x 19 1/2"
SIDE

No. 6 x 3/4"
COUNTERSUNK
BRASS SCREW

2 1/4"

3/4" x 4" x 12"
SLAT SUPPORT

3/8" x 3/4" x 18"
FRONT SLAT

3/4" x 3" x 18"
BOTTOM SHELF

No. 8 x 1" COUNTERSUNK
SCREW

3/8" DOWEL
PLUG

9. Use the No. 8 pilot bit to drill two holes, spaced 1-3/4" apart, through each side to secure the top slat. Set the stop collar at 1-1/4". Fasten with No. 8 x 1" flathead wood screws.

10. Position one 3/8" x 3/4" x 18" slat at the front of the angled supports, flush with their top edges. Use the No. 6 pilot bit to drill a hole at each end. Set the stop collar at 3/4". Then mount the slat with No. 6 x 3/4" flathead brass screws.

11. Fasten a second slat to the supports, flush with the top of the bottom shelf.

12. Space the remaining five slats evenly across the supports; the distance between their edges should be 1-1/8". Drill No. 6 pilot holes; fasten the slats as before.

13. Glue 3/8" dowel plugs into each No. 8 screw bore, sanding them flush once the glue dries.

14. With the No. 8 pilot bit and counterbore, drill two mounting holes through the face of the top slat, centering them to suit your installation needs.

15. Sand the entire project lightly, and finish with several coats of spray lacquer.

135

Clock

Why buy an average looking kitchen clock when you can keep track of the time by constructing an unusual face for a timepiece of your own? The contemporary clock-face project presented here is easy to build; the quartz clockworks (mounted on the back surface) can be purchased in kit form at a hardware store.

Materials List

Walnut, cherry, maple, and oak are recommended for this project.

(1)	3/4" x 2" x 19"	Walnut strip
(2)	3/4" x 1" x 19"	Cherry strips
(2)	3/4" x 1-1/2" x 19"	Maple strips
(2)	3/4" x 1-3/8" x 19"	Maple strips
(2)	3/4" x 1-1/2" x 19"	Maple strips
(1)	3/4" x 3/4" x 16"	Oak cross strips
(1)	3/4" x 2"	Birch dowel

Suggested Tools

3/8" drill
No. 8 pilot bit and countersink with stop collar
5/16" drill bit
3/4" Forstner bit
Router
45° 5/8" chamfer bit
Pipe clamps
Jigsaw
36" straightedge
Compass
Try square
Palm sander
Coping saw
No. 2 Phillips screwdriver
Tack hammer

Hardware & Supplies

Quartz clockworks
Yellow wood glue
No. 8 x 1" flathead wood screws
Spray lacquer

Construction Procedure

1. The face of the clock is made from strips of walnut, cherry, and maple, which are glued together to create a board 3/4" thick. Place the walnut in the center, and a cherry strip on either side of it. To each side of the cherry strips, there are three strips of maple; the 1-3/8" pieces are placed next to the cherry strips.

2. Spread glue evenly on the edges of the strips to be joined, and clamp them squarely. Use a square to check for level. Allow the glue to dry overnight, and then sand both surfaces.

3. Cut the ends square so that the board measures 12-3/4" x 18" overall.

4. Locate the center of the board's width, and strike a lengthwise center line at this point.

5. Measure 6" from one 12-3/4" edge, and mark on the center line. Strike a circle with a 4-1/2" radius at this point. Mark a line across the board at the center of this circle (see Face Layout).

6. At each of the four points where the lines and circle intersect, use a 3/4" Forstner bit to drill a 1/4"-deep hole.

7. With a coping saw, cut four 1/4" lengths from the 3/4"-diameter dowel. Glue them into the sockets

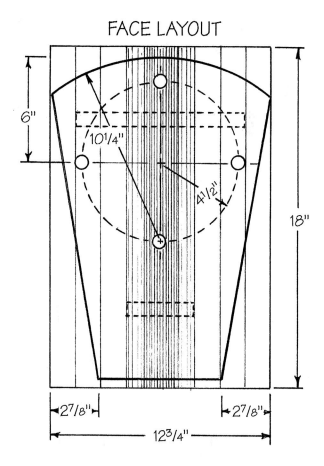

FACE LAYOUT

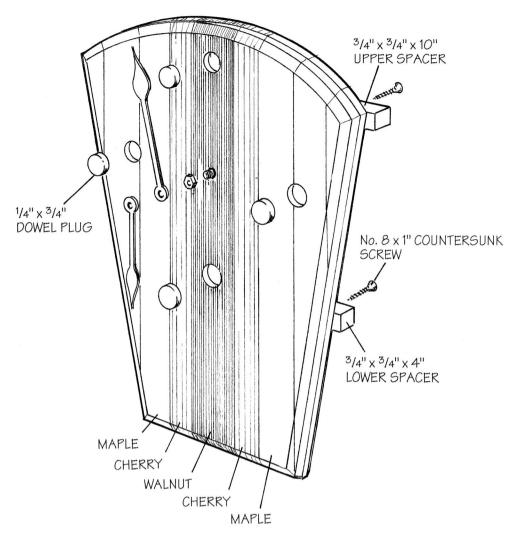

¾" x ¾" x 10"
UPPER SPACER

¼" x ¾"
DOWEL PLUG

No. 8 x 1" COUNTERSUNK
SCREW

¾" x ¾" x 4"
LOWER SPACER

MAPLE

CHERRY

WALNUT

CHERRY

MAPLE

just completed; then sand the dowels flush to the face of the board.

8. Measure 10-3/4" from the original 12-3/4" edge, and mark at the center line. Strike a 10-1/4" radius from this point at the board's top edge.

9. At the bottom of the board, measure and mark 2-7/8" in from each edge. To locate the diagonal edges of the clock's face, strike a line from each of these points to the ends of the 10-1/4" radius above.

10. Use a jigsaw to cut the outline of the clock's face.

11. Using the 45° chamfer bit, rout the board's face edges to a depth of 1/2". Sand the edges smooth.

12. On the board's back face, measure 3-1/2" from the top edge, and 4" from the bottom edge, marking lines across the width.

13. Cut the 3/4" x 16" piece into two strips, 4" and 10" in length.

14. Center the longer strip at the top line and the shorter one at the bottom line. Use the No. 8 pilot bit, with its stop collar set at 1", to drill holes through the strips and into the back face. Fasten the strips with No. 8 x 1" flathead screws.

15. Finish the wood with several coats of spray lacquer.

16. Drill a 5/16" hole through the face board at the circle's center point. Use this hole to mount the clock-works, as described in the instructions packed with the kit.

17. Many clockworks include a metal tab for mounting purposes, but if yours doesn't, you can mount your clock with either picture-hanging wire or a picture-mount (a small piece of metal) attached to the upper cross strip.

Plant Stand

We designed this plant stand for a kitchen corner too small to accept a cabinet or closet and too large to ignore. Favorite houseplants add a bit of greenery to our kitchen, but you can just as easily use the stand's shelves to store mixing bowls, freshly laundered linen towels, and even small appliances. If you need more storage space, go ahead and add another slatted shelf.

Materials List

Cypress is recommended for this project.

(12)	3/4" x 1-1/2" x 12"	Slats
(4)	3/4" x 2-1/2" x 42"	Legs
(4)	3/4" x 2-1/2" x 12"	Supports
(4)	3/4" x 2-1/2" x 10-1/2"	Supports

Suggested Tools

3/8" drill
No. 6 pilot bit and countersink with stop collar
No. 8 pilot bit and countersink with stop collar
Router
3/8" roundover bit
No. 2 Phillips screwdriver
36" straightedge
Square
Palm sander

Hardware & Supplies

Waterproof wood glue
No. 8 x 1" flathead wood screws
No. 6 x 1" flathead brass wood screws
3/8" dowel plugs
Spray polyurethane

Construction Procedure

1. Assemble the upper and lower 12"-square support frames by gluing and fastening the 2-1/2" x 12" pieces to the ends of the 2-1/2" x 10-1/2" pieces. Using the No. 8 pilot bit, drill holes 1-1/4" apart and placed vertically through the face of each 12" piece. Set the stop collar at 1-1/4". Fasten the pieces together with

No. 8 x 1" flathead screws, and then sand the supports' faces. (See the lower, right-hand portion of the illustration for correct placement of screws.)

2. Use a 3/8" roundover bit in the router to round the two face edges of each 2-1/2" x 42" leg. Sand smooth.

3. Fasten the four legs to one of the 12"-square support frames so that the upper ends of the legs are flush with the upper edge of the frame. Glue and place the legs to cover the frame's screw holes. Drill two holes (horizontally) in each leg, 1-1/4" apart. (See the upper, right-hand portion of the illustration for correct placement of screws.) Use the No. 8 pilot bit with the stop collar set at 1-1/4". Fasten with No. 8 x 1" flathead screws.

4. Mount six 1-1/2" x 12" slats to the remaining 12"-square frame, using No. 6 x 1" flathead brass screws. Position one slat at each end of the frame, edges flush, and drill a No. 6 pilot hole through each end of the slats' faces and into the center of the frame

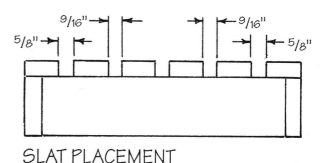

SLAT PLACEMENT

members. Set the stop collar at 1-1/8" to give the screw heads a slight recess once they're driven. Attach the next two adjoining slats 5/8" from the ones already fastened; fasten the final two slats 9/16" from those (see Slat Placement). Sand the assembly.

5. Fasten the assembled lower frame so that its surface is 17" above the bottom of the legs. Use the same gluing and fastening method as that used to attach the upper frame.

6. Attach the remaining six slats to the upper frame, using No. 6 x 1" flathead brass screws; position the slats as in Step 4.

7. Plug all the No. 8 screw holes with 3/8" dowel plugs glued in place. Sand the plugs flush with the surface of the wood; then sand the upper slats smooth.

8. Finish the entire stand with several coats of UV-resistant spray polyurethane.

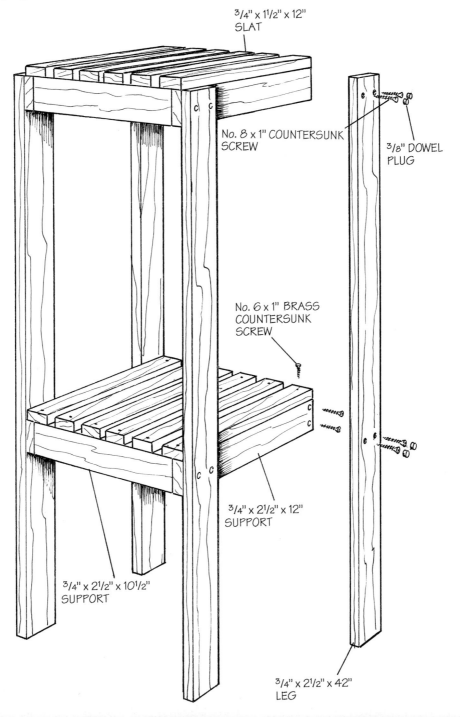

3/4" x 1½" x 12"
SLAT

No. 8 x 1" COUNTERSUNK
SCREW

3/8" DOWEL
PLUG

No. 6 x 1" BRASS
COUNTERSUNK
SCREW

3/4" x 2½" x 12"
SUPPORT

3/4" x 2½" x 10½"
SUPPORT

3/4" x 2½" x 42"
LEG

Plant Table

Cooks who like to use fresh herbs will love this spacious plant table. Its slatted surface is designed to hold either trays or pots of year-round greenery, and its raised edges will keep your plants from tipping over onto the clean kitchen floor. Of course, you don't have to limit your indoor gardening to basil and dill; add a few houseplants and start some seedlings for your spring garden, too.

Materials List

Cherry and white pine are recommended for this project.

(2)	5/8" x 4-1/4" x 44"	Pine side frames
(2)	5/8" x 4-1/4" x 18"	Pine end frames
(4)	5/8" x 1" x 19-5/8"	Pine side supports
(1)	5/8" x 3-1/2" x 18"	Pine center support
(2)	5/8" x 1" x 16"	Pine end supports
(13)	5/8" x 1" x 42-3/4"	Pine table slats
(2)	5/8" x 1-3/4" x 14-1/2"	Cherry upper trim boards
(2)	5/8" x 1-3/4" x 39-1/4"	Cherry upper trim boards
(2)	5/8" x 5/8" x 14-1/2"	Cherry lower trim boards
(2)	5/8" x 5/8" x 39-1/4"	Cherry lower trim boards
(4)	5/8" x 3" x 30"	Pine legs
(4)	5/8" x 2-3/8" x 30"	Pine legs
(2)	5/8" x 3" x 18"	Pine end caps
(2)	5/8" x 3" x 48-3/4"	Pine side caps

Suggested Tools

3/8" drill
No. 6 pilot bit and countersink with stop collar
No. 8 pilot bit and countersink with stop collar
Router
3/8" roundover bit
36" straightedge
No. 2 Phillips screwdriver
Palm sander
Square

Hardware & Supplies

Waterproof wood glue
No. 8 x 1" flathead wood screws
No. 8 x 1-1/4" flathead wood screws
No. 6 x 1" flathead brass wood screws
3/8" dowel plugs
Spray polyurethane

Construction Procedure

1. Fasten the 5/8" x 1" x 19-5/8" side supports flush to one edge of each 4-1/4" x 44" side frame. The ends of the side supports should be 5/8" from the side frames' ends, creating a 3-1/2" notch in the center of each frame piece. Attach the supports by their 5/8" edges, using No. 8 x 1" flathead screws spaced 6" apart. Use the No. 8 pilot bit to bore the holes, and set the stop collar at 1". Sand the faces of both side frames.

2. Fasten the 5/8" x 1" x 16" end supports flush to one edge of each 4-1/4" x 18" end frame. Allow a space of 1" at both ends of each board. Attach the end supports in the same manner as before, but space the screws 7" apart. Sand the end frames' faces.

3. Attach the 44" side frames to the 18" end frames with two No. 8 x 1-1/4" flathead screws; space these 2-1/4" apart at each joint. Use a No. 8 pilot bit, and set the stop collar at 1-1/4". The edges of the end and side frames should be flush with one another, and all supports should be aligned.

4. Slip the 3-1/2" x 18" center support into the frame's center notches. With the No. 8 pilot bit, drill holes 1-1/2" apart through the side frames. Set the stop collar at 1-1/4", and fasten the center support with No. 8 x 1-1/4" flathead screws.

5. Sand the sides and faces of the thirteen 1" x 42-3/4" table slats. Mount a slat to each side support, flush against the side frames, using a No. 6 x 1" flathead brass screw at each end and in the center. Drill the holes with a No. 6 pilot bit; set the stop collar at 1". Attach ten more slats, each 3/8" apart, working toward the center; the thirteenth slat will be 1/2" from those adjacent. Fasten them all in the same manner.

6. Assemble each of the four legs by fastening a 3" x 30" piece to the edge of a 2-3/8" x 30" piece. Use No. 8 x 1" flathead screws, spaced 8" apart and inserted through the faces of the 3" pieces into the edges of the 2-3/8" pieces. Drill the holes with a No. 8 pilot bit, and set the stop collar at 1-1/4".

7. Fasten the legs to the assembled frame so that the tops of the legs and the frame's upper edges are flush. Use No. 8 x 1" flathead screws spaced vertically, 2-1/4" apart, at each leg face. Drill the holes with a No. 8 pilot bit, and set the stop collar at 1-1/8".

8. Mount the four end and side caps to the top edge of the table so that their inner edges are flush with the inside faces of the frame pieces. Drill No. 8 pilot holes 1-1/4" deep through the surface frame and into the edges of the frame. Space the holes 8-1/4" apart on all pieces, and fasten the caps with No. 8 x 1" flathead screws.

9. Plug all the counterbored No. 8 screw holes with 3/8" dowel plugs glued in place. Sand these flush with the surface of the wood.

10. Use a 3/8" roundover bit in the router to round the inside and outside edges of the side and end caps. Sand the edges and surfaces.

11. Round both edges on one face of all the cherry trim boards, and sand them well.

12. Fasten the two 1-3/4" x 14-1/2" and the two 1-3/4" x 39-1/4" upper trim boards against the under faces of the end and side caps. Use a No. 8 x 1" flat-head screw at the ends of each strip. Drill the holes with a No. 8 pilot bit, and set the stop collar at 1-1/4".

13. Fasten the two 5/8" x 14-1/2" and the two 5/8" x 39-1/4" lower trim boards flush with the bottom edges of the end and side frames, using the same method as in Step 12.

14. Plug all the screw holes in the trim board with 3/8" glued dowel plugs, and sand the plugs flush with the wood's surface.

15. Go over the entire table, sanding any rough surfaces. Finish the table with a UV-resistant spray polyurethane

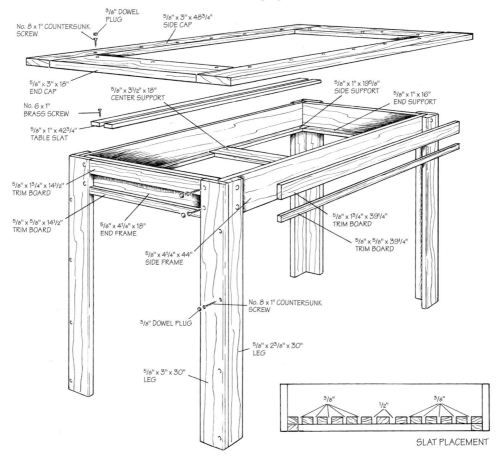

Trash-Bin Container

Plastic garbage bins are effective, but they're often downright ugly. Maybe that's why people tend to hide them under the sink. For folks who hate bending over to open a cabinet door every time they want to throw away a used paper towel, though, this project provides the ideal solution. Designed to fit—and hide—a standard-sized, plastic bin, its lift-up lid makes trash disposal an easy matter.

Materials List

Maple is recommended for this project.

(2)	3/4" x 16" x 27-7/8"	Side panels
(2)	3/4" x 12-1/2" x 27-7/8"	Front and rear panels
(1)	3/4" x 12-1/2" x 16"	Lid
(2)	3/4" x 3/4" x 12-1/2"	Lid end strips
(1)	3/4" x 10-15/16" x 16"	Bottom
(2)	5/8" x 3/4" x 16"	Lid guide strips
(2)	3/4" x 2"	Birch dowels
(1)	1" x 12"	Birch dowel

Suggested Tools

3/8" drill
No. 6 pilot bit and countersink with stop collar
No. 8 pilot bit and countersink with stop collar
3/4" spade bit
Router
3/8" roundover bit
Pipe clamps
Square
36" straightedge
Palm sander
No. 2 Phillips screwdriver
Tack hammer

Hardware & Supplies

Yellow wood glue
No. 8 x 1" flathead wood screws
No. 6 x 3/4" flathead wood screws
18-gauge x 3/4" brads
3/8" dowel plugs
Spray polyurethane

Construction Procedure

1. If necessary, glue up strips of maple to achieve the required dimensions. Spread glue along the edges of the strips to be joined, and clamp them securely. Use the square to check for a level surface; then allow the glue to dry overnight. When the glue has dried, trim the boards to the proper dimensions, and sand both faces and the edges.

2. Glue a 3/4" x 3/4" x 12-1/2" strip to each end of the 16" lid to bring the board's final dimensions to 12-1/2" x 17-1/2". Glue these strips with their grain running perpendicular to the lengthwise grain of the center piece (see Lid Detail).

3. Fasten the two 12-1/2" x 27-7/8" front and rear panels to the edges of the two 16" x 27-7/8" side panels, flush with the sides. Use a No. 8 pilot bit to drill holes 8" apart, and set the depth stop at 1-1/4". Fasten with No. 8 x 1" flathead screws. (Work each joint from one end to the other, as this will enable you to straighten the wood if it's slightly warped.)

4. Mount the 10-15/16" x 16" bottom piece 1/4" from the lower edge of the box frame by driving No. 8 x 1" flathead wood screws from the outside. The bottom is cut slightly narrow to allow an easy fit, though you can sand the edges if it's still tight. Use a No. 8 pilot bit, setting the stop collar at 1-1/4", and space the screws 8" apart.

5. On the 12-1/2" x 17-1/2" lid, measure in 3/4" from the ends and edges and strike lines. Mount the two 5/8" x 3/4" x 16" guide strips at the inside edges of the marked borders, using No. 6 x 3/4" flathead wood screws spaced 7" apart (see Lid Detail). Use a No. 6 pilot bit with the stop collar set at 3/4" to drill the mounting holes.

6. Measure 3" in from each end of the 1" x 12" dowel, and mark at the center of the dowel's diameter. At each point, drill a 3/4" hole, 3/8" deep.

LID DETAIL

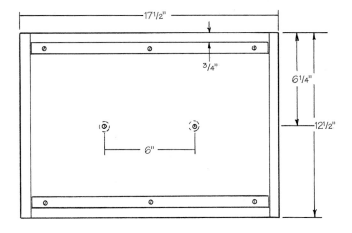

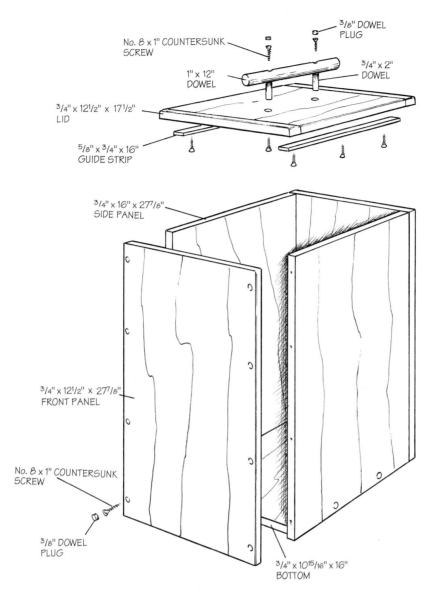

No. 8 x 1" COUNTERSUNK SCREW

3/8" DOWEL PLUG

1" x 12" DOWEL

3/4" x 2" DOWEL

3/4" x 12 1/2" x 17 1/2" LID

5/8" x 3/4" x 16" GUIDE STRIP

3/4" x 16" x 27 7/8" SIDE PANEL

3/4" x 12 1/2" x 27 7/8" FRONT PANEL

No. 8 x 1" COUNTERSUNK SCREW

3/8" DOWEL PLUG

3/4" x 10 15/16" x 16" BOTTOM

7. Fasten the two 3/4" x 2" dowels in these holes by drilling holes through the opposite side of the 1" dowel with the No. 8 pilot bit. Set the stop collar at 1-1/4". Drive 3/4" brads through the larger dowel's sides to keep the smaller dowels from rotating, and fasten with No. 8 x 1" flathead wood screws.

8. Strike a center line down the length and width of the lid's bottom face. Measure 3" to each side of the lid's center, along the lengthwise line, and mark. Use a No. 8 pilot bit to drill from the bottom face and into the 3/4" handle dowels. Set the stop collar at 1-1/4".

9. Use the 3/4" bit to make 1/8"-deep sockets in the lid's upper surface at the handle-mounting holes.

10. With a 3/8" roundover bit in the router, round all the lid's face edges. Then mount the handle with No. 8 x 1" flathead screws.

11. Plug all the external screw holes with 3/8" dowel plugs glued in place. Sand these flush with the wood's surface.

12. Use the 3/8" roundover bit to round all the outside corners, including the ones at the top and bottom edges.

13. Sand the wood lightly.

14. Finish the project with several coats of spray polyurethane.

Recycling Bin

Recycling doesn't have to be a messy or time-consuming chore. Place a garbage can liner in this surprisingly large bin, drop your cans, glass jars, or newspapers in it every day, and hide the contents by closing the hinged lid. When the bin is full, just lift the bag out, and tote its contents to the nearest recycling center. Don't forget to recycle that plastic liner too!

Materials List

White pine is recommended for this project.

(2)	3/4" x 20" x 20"	Sides
(1)	3/4" x 15-1/2" x 15-3/4"	Lid
(1)	3/4" x 14" x 20"	Back
(1)	3/4" x 5-3/4" x 15-1/2"	Top
(1)	3/4" x 14" x 14-3/4"	Front
(1)	3/4" x 14" x 18-1/2"	Bottom

Suggested Tools

3/8" drill
No. 8 pilot bit and countersink with stop collar
Router
3/8" roundover bit
Circular saw
36" straightedge
No. 2 Phillips screwdriver
Palm sander
Pipe clamps

Hardware & Supplies

Yellow wood glue
No. 8 x 1-1/4" flathead wood screws
4" strap hinges (2)
Spray polyurethane

Construction Procedure

1. Glue up sections of 3/4" pine board to create the stock indicated in the list above. Use pipe clamps to hold the boards while the glue sets.

2. With a circular saw, trim the pieces to the proper dimensions. On one side piece, make a mark

5-3/4" from the top of the right 20" edge and another mark 14-3/4" from the bottom of the lower 20" edge (see Side Layout). Strike a line between the two marks.

3. Clamp the two 20"-square boards together. Then cut along the marked line to remove the corners of both. Sand the cut edges.

4. Fasten the 14" x 20" back between the two sides so that the outer face of the back is flush with the sides' edges. With the No. 8 pilot bit and a stop collar set at 1-1/2", drill holes 6" apart, 3/8" in from each side's edge. Use No. 8 x 1-1/4" flathead wood screws to secure the joints.

5. Fasten the 14" x 14-3/4" front between the two sides in the same manner. Space the screws 4-1/4" apart.

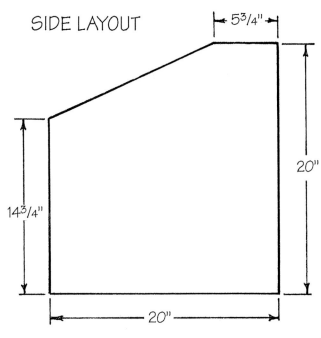

SIDE LAYOUT

6. Fasten the 5-3/4" x 15-1/2" top to the box's upper edges so that the top's three edges are flush with the sides and back. Drill and screw in place as before. Space the screws 3-3/4" apart on the sides and 4-1/2" apart along the back edge.

7. Slip the 14" x 18-1/2" bottom board in place, recessing it 1/4" from the bottom edge. Mark, drill, and fasten it from the outside. The side screws should be 4-1/2" apart, and the front and back ones 4" apart.

8. Plug all the screw holes with 3/8" dowel plugs glued in place. Sand the plugs flush with the surface.

9. Using a 3/8" roundover bit in the router, rout all the assembly's outside edges.

10. On the 15-1/2" x 15-3/4" lid, use the same technique to round all the inside and outside edges except one inside edge on either 15-1/2" end.

11. With the circular saw blade set at 25°, cut the square 15-1/2" edge to that angle so that this edge of the lid matches the top when the lid is mounted.

12. Fasten the lid in place with two 4" strap hinges, using the hardware provided. Position each hinge 3" in from the side.

13. Sand the completed bin lightly. Finish with several coats of spray polyurethane.

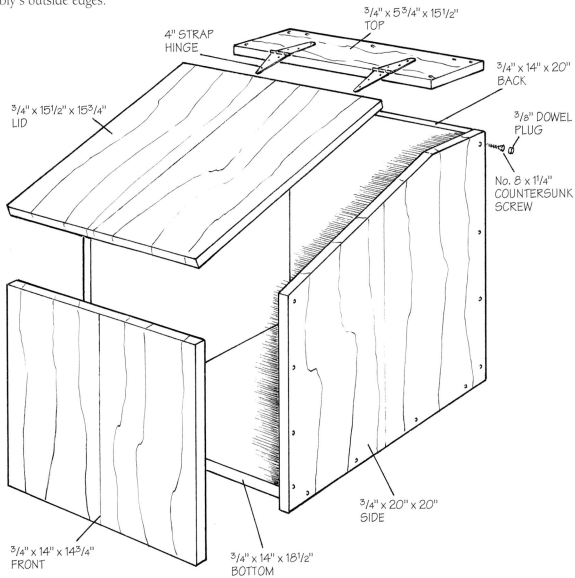

4" STRAP HINGE

3/4" x 5 3/4" x 15 1/2" TOP

3/4" x 14" x 20" BACK

3/8" DOWEL PLUG

3/4" x 15 1/2" x 15 3/4" LID

No. 8 x 1 1/4" COUNTERSUNK SCREW

3/4" x 20" x 20" SIDE

3/4" x 14" x 14 3/4" FRONT

3/4" x 14" x 18 1/2" BOTTOM

Acknowledgements

Many thanks to

Richard Freudenberger, Executive Editor of *Back Home* magazine, for his invaluable help with writing

Mike Hester, owner of Hester's Lothlorien, for his support and encouragement

Henry Lanz of Garrett Wade Company, Inc., for permission to use the photograph on page 9

Raymond McClinton, for the loan of his workshop

Don Osby, owner of Page 1 Publications, for his illustrations

Elaine Thompson, for her skills and (almost) limitless patience

Thanks also to the following residents of Asheville, NC, for their help with location photography:

Deborah S. and Michael H. Buck

Julie and Bruce Howerton

Judith Lally (Beverly-Hanks & Associates)

Kathryn S. Long (Ambiance Interiors)

Sue and Raymond McClinton

Carol Parks

Sharon Tompkins (Tompkins-Jones Painting Studio)

METRIC EQUIVALENCY CHART

LINEAR

INCHES	CM	INCHES	CM
1/8	0.3	26	66.0
1/4	0.6	27	68.6
3/8	1.0	28	71.1
1/2	1.3	29	73.7
5/8	1.6	30	76.2
3/4	1.9	31	78.7
7/8	2.2	32	81.3
1	2.54	33	83.8
1-1/4	3.2	34	86.4
1-1/2	3.8	35	88.9
1-3/4	4.4	36	91.44
2	5.1	37	94.0
2-1/2	6.4	38	96.5
3	7.6	39	99.1
3-1/2	8.9	40	101.6
4	10.2	41	104.1
4-1/2	11.4	42	106.7
5	12.7	43	109.2
6	15.2	44	111.8
7	17.8	45	114.3
8	20.3	46	116.8
9	22.9	47	119.4
10	25.4	48	121.9
11	27.9	49	124.5
12	30.48	50	127.0
13	33.0		
14	35.6		
15	38.1		
16	40.6		
17	43.2		
18	45.7		
19	48.3		
20	50.8		
21	53.3		
22	55.9		
23	58.4		
24	61.0		
25	63.5		

CAPACITY

1 pint = .568 litres
1 quart = 1.136 litres
1 gallon = 4.546 litres

WEIGHT

1 ounce = 28.35 grams
1 pound = 0.4536 kilograms

SOFTWOOD SIZES

NOMINAL	ACTUAL
1 x 2	3/4" x 1-1/2"
1 x 3	3/4" x 2-1/2"
1 x 4	3/4" x 3-1/2"
1 x 5	3/4" x 4-1/2"
1 x 6	3/4" x 5-1/2"
1 x 8	3/4" x 7-1/4"
1 x 10	3/4" x 9-1/4"
1 x 12	3/4" x 11-1/4"
2 x 2	1-1/2" x 1-1/2"
2 x 4	1-1/2" x 3-1/2"
2 x 6	1-1/2" x 5-1/2"
2 x 8	1-1/2" x 7-1/4"
2 x 10	1-1/2" x 9-1/4"
2 x 12	1-1/2" x 11-1/4"
4 x 4	3-1/2" x 3-1/2"
4 x 6	3-1/2" x 5-1/2"
6 x 6	5-1/2" x 5-1/2"
8 x 8	7-1/2" x 7-1/2"

Index